The Circle of Life

Healthy habits to build your faith

Dr Roger Aubrey

xulon
PRESS

The Circle of Life
by Dr. Roger Aubrey

Printed in the United States of America

ISBN 978-1-60266-185-1

www.xulonpress.com

For Dianne, Naomi, James and Saskia
Just happy to be here because of you.

Table of Contents

Acknowledgments

The material that eventually found its way into this book originated as a teaching series in my home church over a period of two years. My grateful thanks, therefore, to the people of God at All Nations Church in Cardiff, Wales for listening to and living out the Word. They are the best people in the world and proof that what's in this book works. Thanks to Keri Jones, my father in the faith, who has taught me more than anybody else, how to live in positive confession. I really appreciate the valued input of Annie Sherwin, who read the manuscript meticulously and gave me so much helpful feedback and encouragement to go ahead with publishing what you have in your hand. Thanks also to my great friend Andrew Hughes for his suggestions and encouragement to get on with writing instead of just talking about it. Most of all, thanks to my family: to my son James for putting his PhD skills to use, editing the text and hauling it into something readable while still in the first flush of marriage to his wonderful wife Saskia. Thanks to my incredible daughter Naomi for giving the finished work her seal of approval. The biggest thank you as always belongs to my wife Dianne, who not only was my soundboard and muse, but who personifies what this book teaches. 'You're the red in my painting.'

INTRODUCTION

The Circle of Life

Some years ago there was a famous football (soccer) coach here in the UK called Bill Shankly. He had a very simple philosophy concerning football: it is a beautiful game and should be played simply. He believed that if his team, Liverpool, did the simple things well, they would become the best. Shankly's philosophy paid off. He built a football club that for most of the 1970's and 80's was one of the best in the world.

Christianity is very simple. I know it contains the most profound and amazing truths; it challenges the natural mind. To believe in a triune God, that God is one in three and three in one defies the logic of rational people: but it is true. Nevertheless, I believe it's simple to live the Christian life and God has given us all the resources we need to live. The Bible helps us in very practical ways, giving us principles of faith we are meant to live by. If we put them into practice then we will be blessed and have wonderful and fulfilled lives. After all, God is a good God and he wants his children to be blessed and to be a blessing.

My aim is to help you live the simple and uncomplicated life of faith. I believe God has designed us as new creations in Christ to live by faith; therefore it's natural for us to do so. Certainly it demands commitment, but it's not meant to be attained only by a select few. Anybody who knows Jesus can do it. The Word of God gives us a simple, fourfold process of living by faith; if we adopt it as a lifestyle it will revolutionise our lives and churches. All we have to do is learn how to hear, believe, confess and do the Word of God. It's that easy.

I call this process of hearing, believing, confessing and doing the *Circle of Life* and I am going to share it with you. I know it will help you. Please read on and be blessed.

CHAPTER ONE

Act naturally

Whoever you are, wherever you are, right now you're doing the same thing every person in the world is doing: you're breathing.

You were probably not even aware of the fact until I mentioned it; breathing is just something that you've been doing from the moment you entered the world. Sometimes you're more conscious that you're breathing than at other times: after running for the bus, when you realise you're not as fit as you thought; or when you dive into the swimming pool, holding your breath for as long as you can underwater and then bursting through to the surface again, taking vast gulps of fresh air into your lungs. But more often than not, thousands of times each day, you just breathe. It comes naturally.

God has designed us as human beings to be natural breathers, not those who take an occasional breath, or who hold our breath until we pass out. Neither do we have to remind ourselves to breathe. I don't wake up each morning and include 'remember to breathe' on my to-do list for the day. It's just natural for me to breathe. Because God has designed us in such a wonderful way, he provides all the air we need as human beings in order to live. He doesn't ration the air, limiting us so that we are allowed to breathe just one day a week; there's always more than enough air for everybody in the whole world, with plenty to spare. Air has a specific purpose: in the air that we take into our bodies is the very thing we need to live — oxygen.

Breathing is important — vitally important. In fact, it's a matter of life and death. If we stop breathing we die, simple as that. I remember once when a friend of mine collapsed unconscious. The first thing those of us around him did was to check that he was still breathing. We had to ensure that his airways were clear. If he'd stopped breathing in just a few minutes his brain would have been irreversibly damaged and he would have died. Happily he came around with no ill effects.

For Christians, living by faith is just as natural and just as vital as breathing. In the same way that breathing air is natural, so for the Christian is living by faith. The Bible says that *'the righteous live by faith'* (Romans 1:17). We don't just survive or get by on it, we live by it. In the same way that our natural bodies thrive on air, God has designed all who are in Christ to live by faith. We don't have to take the occasional gulp of faith and struggle through, holding our 'breath' and becoming spiritually dizzy, hoping that there will be a little bit more for us one day. Neither do we panic and stockpile our faith in case it runs out, (although I will show you later how we can build it). No, in the same way we breathe the air around us unconsciously, we live every moment of life by faith. Faith is like oxygen: there's plenty of it around and all you have to do is 'breathe'. Living by faith is the easiest thing in the world for a Christian to do. And it's important: Hebrews 11:6 says that *'without faith it's impossible to please God.'* Therefore, if for no other reason than it pleases God, I'll be a man of faith.

God knows we need faith, just like we need the air to breathe. He is such a good and generous God that he gives us all the faith we need:

> *It is by grace you have been saved, through faith—and this not from yourselves, it is the gift of God. (Ephesians 2:8)*

Imagine that: God knows that for us to live we need faith, so he gives us all the faith we need in order to please him and fulfil all that he created us for. He doesn't sit back on his throne in Heaven, waiting for us to struggle through life, trying to get faith; he gives it to us. That is why it is easy to live by faith.

A young lady approached me when I was teaching at a conference on faith. She asked me this question: 'Why doesn't God make it easy for us to trust him? Why does he say we have to have faith?' I thought about this for a few moments; it was a very good question. Then I replied, 'But God *has* made it easy; he's given us all the faith we need to trust him. That is how he has designed us as his children: to know him by faith.' I realised that this young lady was like so many Christians: they are unaware of just what God has made available to them in giving them faith. There is a vast untapped resource of faith that is yet to be released in the lives of thousands of God's people.

That's why I decided to write this book; on the following pages I want to share with you how easy and natural it is for you to live by faith. Over recent years I have progressively learnt the *Circle of Life* that is living by faith. It has not only revolutionised my life; on one occasion it actually saved my life. I'll tell you all about that later on; for now let's begin by discovering what faith is.

CHAPTER TWO

What is faith?

We live by faith and not by sight. (2Corinthians 5:7)

Many of us are raised and taught to trust only in what we can see or prove by reason. We are told to rely only on our natural senses: sight, sound, touch, smell and taste. But in many areas of life we exercise a kind of faith all the time. Have you ever been on a plane? You board an aircraft that in a few minutes will soar 35,000 feet into the air. Behind a door at the front sits somebody you have never met nor know anything about. The stewardess might tell you the pilot's name, but you don't meet them face to face. You take the stewardess' word for it that the pilot is there. You don't check credentials or demand an interview with the pilot so they can convince you they can actually fly. It's possible you might hear a voice that says, 'This is your captain speaking.' You don't question it. You merely sit back in your seat, maybe put on the movie or get out your book, and relax. The plane takes off and a few hours later it lands. That's a certain kind of faith and we exercise it every day in many different ways. Bible faith, however, is much more than that.

Why do we need faith? The answer is very simple: while God is real, as real as anything you can see, he is invisible. You can't see God, but he's really there. How can you see someone who can't be seen? By faith. Our natural senses are God-given and necessary for us to live as human beings: the sight of a sunset is staggering; the sound of a beautiful piece of music can move you to tears. But when it comes to knowing God we have to rely on something more than our natural senses: we must have faith. Since faith is so vital if we are to know God, the very first thing we have to do in establishing how to live the *Circle of Life* is to discover what the Bible means when it talks about faith.

What is faith?

> *Now faith is the substance of things hoped for, the evidence of things not seen. (Hebrews 11:1 KJV)*

Since the Bible gives us such a clear definition of faith, let's examine each part of this verse in greater detail.

Now FAITH is the substance of things hoped for, the evidence of things not seen.

In the New Testament the words 'faith', 'believe' and 'trust' are often translated from the same Greek word (*pistis*). This word literally means:

> *An absolute conviction; being one hundred percent convinced, having no doubt at all. To believe completely something you **heard**.*

First of all, then, **faith is hearing somebody say something and believing or trusting completely what that person has said**. Right at the beginning we see something that we'll have to develop later on: at its very root, faith is all about hearing. The Bible confirms this:

> *Faith comes from hearing, and hearing through the Word of Christ. (Romans 10:17)*

Faith is not static; it comes to you. And it comes in a specific and unique way: by hearing. The word the New Testament uses for *hearing* means much more than just hearing words with your natural ears; it literally means:

To receive words into your heart (the inner man), in order to obey them, do them, live by them, ***and become them.***

Just note this for now: the integrity and trustworthiness of the one who is speaking those words is of utmost importance. The reliability of the speaker is paramount. I hope that by now you're beginning to realise the power of words and the power of hearing. The words you listen to and choose to believe will get right inside you and become part of you. Health experts say you are what you eat; but you are what you listen to and believe.

Now faith is the <u>SUBSTANCE</u> of things hoped for, the evidence of things not seen.

This word (*hupostasis*) means *'that which stands under or provides the basis for something,'* such as the foundation of a building. It is a very strong image and is even used to describe Jesus:

The Son is the radiance of [God's] glory and the representation of ***the reality*** *of him. (Hebrews 1:3, literal translation)*

Jesus is the reality of God; that's why he could say, *'If you have seen me you have seen the Father'* (John 14:9).

In ancient times a *hupostasis* was a document or a title deed to a piece of land or property. It was the proof that the person who claimed to own the land really did. We have the same practice today: I own my home and I have the title deeds to my house and the land it stands on. Imagine I arrive home after being away on holiday for a week. As I drive into the street I discover that a car I don't recognise is parked in the drive and all the lights are on in the house. I walk through the front door to find that total strangers are sitting on my sofa, eating my food, watching my television. I say to them, 'What on earth are you doing in my home?' and they reply, 'This is our house; we live here. We own it.' I don't need to get into any panic or argument. I just go to my study and bring out my *hupostasis.* It has the name of the property and my name on it; there is the official stamp and seal of all the legal authorities proving it's mine. I take it back to the illegal intruders, wave it in front of them as proof of my ownership and drive them out. They have no legal basis for their claim and must go. But I have a legal claim to my house and my *hupostasis* proves it.

That's what faith is: it's like having a legal title deed to a piece of property. And the legal authority behind it is the one who has all authority, Almighty God! Faith guarantees the reality of something; it isn't empty theory, but the real substance, the actual reality of what we have heard God say and believe him for.

Now faith is the substance <u>OF THINGS</u> hoped for, the evidence of things not seen.

'Keeping it real.' That's what this word (*pragma*) is all about; it means *'something that has been done'* and we get our English word *pragmatic* from it. To be pragmatic is to be practical, down to earth, and real. Pragmatists are concerned with the 'rubber hitting the road;' they want to know if the theory really works.

Faith keeps it real; it's concerned about what is really there. After all, the fact that we cannot see God doesn't mean he doesn't exist. He does exist and he is present everywhere (theologians call this God's omnipresence). God fills every part of the universe and he exists beyond it:

Where can I go from your Spirit? Where can I flee from your presence? (Psalm 139:7)

God is closer to you right now than your own skin; you can't see him, but he's really there. Have you ever wondered how crazy your worship looks to non-Christians? There you stand, with your hands raised to the sky, your head raised, your mouth filled with songs of praise and adoration, loving somebody you can't see. But you knew all the time that the God you've never seen was really there didn't you?

Jesus said,

I tell you, whatever you ask for in prayer, believe that you ***have*** *received it, and it will be yours. (Mark 11:24)*

Jesus didn't say, 'Believe you **will** receive it,' he said, 'Believe you **have** received it.' As far as God is concerned whatever you ask for already exists; it is a 'real thing' already. Faith is not wishful thinking: your prayer is already answered, and you already have the 'thing' you had faith God would provide.

Now faith is the substance of things HOPED FOR, the evidence of things not seen.

I live in Wales where the national sport is Rugby Union. In the 1970's our team was the best in the world, with some of the greatest players of all time in the side. In those days I never doubted that they would win, and win well.

Nowadays it's rather different because the Welsh team are sadly no longer world beaters. Each time they take the field I hope they will win, but I also have that nagging doubt that they're going to lose. All too often my doubts are well founded. Many people live like this in other, more important areas of their lives. They hope for the best but at the same time they're crossing their fingers, touching wood, and grasping a rabbit's tail, just in case. Christians live like this in the way they express their faith: 'I hope I will be healed;' 'I hope God provides my need;' 'I hope that I'll have enough food and money to feed the family;' 'I hope I'll get married.' Such hope is not the hope that works with faith. Biblical hope has no doubt or uncertainty in it. The word (*elpis*) actually means:

The certain expectation of eventual good; a confident and unswerving expectation that all will be well.

Hope is an important aspect of faith, because you can't have one without the other. Hope deals with the ultimate future and faith brings that future into the present. This total confidence for the future undergirds faith, and as a result faith brings that unswerving expectation of eventual good from the future into the present. As Hebrews 6:19 says: *'we have this hope as an anchor.'*

The example of Abraham

The life of Abraham is a tremendous example of how hope and faith work together. God told Abraham, even though he was seventy five, that he would be the means by which God would bless the whole world (see Genesis 12:1-3). During the following years that word became more specific, culminating in the promise that God would give Abraham and his wife Sarah a son, whose name would be Isaac. There was only one problem — or two, in fact. Abraham was by now a very old man and Sarah, who was ten years younger, was unable to have children. And you think that *you* have problems! But notice how hope and faith worked together in Abraham:

> *Against all **hope**, Abraham in **hope** believed [had **faith**] and so became the father of many nations, just as it had been said to him, "So shall your offspring be." Without weakening in his **faith**, he faced the fact that his body was as good as dead—since he was about a hundred years old—and that Sarah's womb was also dead. Yet he did not waver through unbelief regarding the promise of God, but was strengthened in his **faith** and gave glory to God, being fully persuaded that God had power to do what he had promised. This is why "it was credited to him as righteousness." (Romans 4:18-22)*

This was a naturally hopeless situation. But Abraham had the Bible kind of hope, the confident expectation of the future, that no matter how long it took it would happen. And each year his faith worked with that hope. Notice that instead of becoming more desperate and worried, Abraham actually became stronger in faith as each year passed. Why? Because he had that confident hope of eventual good and his faith worked with it to bring it into the now. He had hope and faith because he believed what God told him: that even though he was an old man and Sarah was barren, an impossible situation would change. How? Simply because God said so, and he was able to deliver on his promise. Twenty five years after God made his initial promise to Abraham, Isaac was born. Has God ever made you a promise? Hold on to hope; the promise is still good.

Now faith is the substance of things hoped for, the <u>EVIDENCE</u> of things not seen.

I am a big fan of the television series *CSI (Crime Scene Investigation).* It's about a team of forensic scientists who work in the crime laboratory of the Las Vegas Police Department. Their job is to attend scenes of crimes and gather evidence to build a case. Each show starts with the crime, and then the team gather evidence so the police can catch the perpetrator and ensure a watertight conviction. The constant advice from Gil Grissom, the leader, to his team is, 'Follow the evidence'. Once they have all the evidence — sometimes just a hair, a partial fingerprint or a tiny speck of blood — they know they have their man. As a result no lawyer will be able to get their client off on some technicality; the evidence proves the case.

That's exactly what evidence (*elegchos*) does: it's the proof of the case. If faith is evidence it must be the proof of something that exists, even though it's unseen. In Bible times this term was used in a legal setting where two opposing parties were in dispute with each other. One brought accusation against the other in order to prove them wrong. The evidence that the defendant brought to court was vital for his case. First of all it established his own innocence absolutely; but more importantly it was so convincing that the evidence proved his accuser wrong, silencing him forever on the matter. It's interesting that the Bible calls the devil 'Satan,' which means *accuser*, and sometimes when he speaks to you he accuses you. But your faith withstands him and shuts him up — for good. But if you believe him...well, we're running ahead of ourselves.

Now faith is the substance of things hoped for, the evidence of things <u>NOT SEEN.</u>

There is an inevitability about this last aspect of faith. If we could see God then we wouldn't need faith; but as we've already said, you can only see the unseen — who is really there — by faith.

That is why *'we fix our eyes not in what is seen but on what is unseen. For what is seen is temporary, but what is unseen is eternal'* (2Corinthians 4:18). Faith must be faith in the unseen God for what is already in existence: that loved one you're praying to be saved; the financial need; the new job; the end of a sickness. It may not be manifested yet, but it's there all the same.

And that's what faith is: **God said it and I believe it**.

Genuine faith needs no other evidence than what God has said. That's why the Bible is so important: it is God's breathed out, spoken word written down (2Timothy 3:16-17). Faith does not need the confirmation of any physical evidence or proof. It does not rely on our natural senses. It is convinced solely by the promise of the One who spoke and speaks. It trusts in the absolute integrity of God and in his ability to perform and do what he has promised. That's all faith needs — nothing else. Faith is convinced just by God's word, which is his integrity. This is the faith God has given us and which he intends us to live by every moment of our lives.

We began this chapter with Hebrews 11:1; let's finish it with the same verse from the New American Standard Bible. Read it a few times before you turn the page and begin the next chapter:

> *Now faith is the assurance (the confirmation, the title deed) of the things [we] hope for, being the proof of things [we] do not see and the conviction of their reality [faith perceiving as real fact what is not revealed to the senses].*

CHAPTER THREE

The God who speaks

Faith comes by hearing. (Romans 10:17)

The tongue has the power of life and death. (Proverbs 18:21)

Take a moment to think of all the voices you have heard today: on the train or bus; at the airport; in the office or school; at the supermarket; on the television or radio; in the newspaper or magazine; in conversations with your family and friends; in the Bible passage you read. That's a lot of words, hundreds of thousands of them, and many voices speaking to you. Even the things you have looked at have spoken to you. *After seeing that commercial you've just got to have the latest model of your mobile phone. How did you ever survive without that shampoo? You must buy that new breakfast cereal. Your life will be poorer if you don't get that new computer with all those gadgets.* Images speak as powerfully as the spoken word. My words on this page are speaking to you right now. Each voice you listen to, spoken or seen, affects you; nothing is neutral. If you let a voice take root in your heart, eventually it will produce fruit. Whatever you put in, whatever you hear and allow to get into your heart will one day come out in your own words and actions. Jesus said, *'Out of the overflow of the heart the mouth speaks'* (Matthew 12:34).

It's of utmost importance, therefore that we guard what we hear. Call to mind some of the things that have been said to you in the course of this past twenty four hours: maybe a teacher ridiculed you in front of the class; perhaps a parent said you were stupid; or somebody called just to encourage you; the doctor said that the tests results are clear; someone said thank you. Every word you hear has the power of life or death in it.

Words have the amazing ability to change lives:

- 'I love you'
- 'Your sickness is terminal'
- 'Will you marry me?'
- 'You've got the job'
- 'I want a divorce'
- 'You're having twins!'
- 'I'm giving you a raise'

There is an old English proverb that says, *'Sticks and stones may break my bones but words will never hurt me'*. That's a lie. I've met far too many people who have been completely destroyed by words. Some years ago a friend of mine (I'll call him John) arrived at our home quite distressed. John needed to talk to my wife Dianne and me. At the time he lived with his parents, but his brother Joe had recently married. A couple of nights previously John had been lying in bed and could hear his mum and dad in conversation in their room. They were talking about their two sons, totally unaware that John could hear them. They spoke warmly about Joe: how proud they were of him; how well he had done in his career; how blessed they felt that he had found a lovely wife. Then they began to speak about John. Their words crushed him: even though they loved him they had never intended to have him. He was a mistake. As this man in his mid twenties sat in my home, weeping and completely devastated by the words of his parents, I took him to the Word of God and showed him from the scriptures that despite what he had heard, there was another voice that had spoken about him long before he was born. John was the apple of God's eye (Psalm 17:8), chosen before the formation of the world (Ephesians 1:11). As the words I was bringing John battled against those of his parents, he decided to believe what the Word of God was speaking to him. The power of those words brought release and freedom to John: today he is happily married to a lady who adores him, with wonderful children he loves with all his heart.

Words have the power to create or destroy; what comes out of our mouths matters.

In the previous chapter we defined faith as believing completely something you have heard. Faith is hearing somebody speak something and believing completely what that person has said. We could say faith is all about hearing. If that is so, it means somebody is speaking to you. In fact, when we really get down to it, every word spoken to us comes from one of two sources. You must understand this: there are only two voices in the universe that speak:

- One always speaks words of life, the other always speaks words of death;
- One always speaks words of faith, the other always speaks words of fear;
- One always speaks the truth, the other always speaks lies;
- One always speaks words of love, the other always speaks words of hate;
- One always speaks words of light, the other always speaks words of darkness;
- One always commends, the other always condemns;
- One always speaks words of clarity, the other always speaks words of confusion;
- One always speaks creatively, the other always speaks destructively;
- One is the voice of God; the other is the voice of the devil.

The Voice of God

In the very first chapter of the Bible we discover that the God who made the universe is a God who speaks. Genesis 1:1 tells us that God created the heavens and the earth; verse three reveals how he did it. He spoke: *'Let there be light.'* Notice that: in order to create, **God said something**. God is the all-powerful Creator, yet he spoke real words in order to create this amazing universe. One hundred billion known galaxies, each with one hundred billion stars, came into being at the spoken word of God:

> *He determines the number of the stars and calls them each by name. (Psalm 147:4)*

> *Lift your eyes and look to the heavens: Who created all these? He who brings out the starry host one by one, and calls them each by name. Because of his great power and mighty strength, not one of them is missing. (Isaiah 40:26)*

A thought was not enough; God did not think the universe into existence. He spoke: 'Light, be' — and there was light. The voice of God has incredible creative power. Before God spoke he didn't think, 'I wonder if it will happen.' He didn't get lucky or find the magic formula; God believed in the power of his spoken word. If you like, God had faith in his own words. Behind that spoken word was the very nature of God himself. He knew that his spoken word, coming from within his being as the Creator God of all power, would work. So he spoke, knowing without a shadow of a doubt that what he called into being would actually come into existence. And it did. God *'calls into existence the things that do not exist'* (Romans 4:17 ESV).

In fact, if you look closely at Genesis 1, you will discover that everything God created he created by speaking. In each individual act of the creation you find God spoke, '*let there be...and there was.*' Every time he spoke something came into being that was not there until he spoke. Other passages in the Word of God remind us of this:

> *By the word of the LORD were the heavens made, their starry host by the breath of his mouth...For* ***he spoke****, and it came to be;* ***he commanded****, and it stood firm. (Psalm 33:6,9)*

> *By faith we understand that the universe was formed at* ***God's command****, so that what is seen was not made out of what was visible. (Hebrews 11:3)*

These are tremendous scriptures; they tell us amazing truth about the creative power of God's voice. When he speaks things are created, because every word God speaks is creative. Just take a moment to look out of the window at the sky right now; it was formed by your heavenly Father's voice. The God who spoke the creation into being still speaks to you today.

Even mankind was created by the spoken word of God. In Genesis 1:26 God spoke to himself and said, *'Let us make man in our image, in our likeness.'* God spoke to himself as Father, Son and Holy Spirit, and in perfect agreement with himself he spoke mankind into being. It is true that man was actually fashioned from the dust of the earth (see Genesis 2:7), but only after God had spoken. That is very important; God was demonstrating to us something vital here about his words: they have creative power. We are going to discover in due course that we need to be speakers of creative words if we're going to live the *Circle of Life*. We will find that our words have the same creative power when we speak agreement with the Word of God.

What did God say about mankind and to mankind?

> *'Let us make man in our image, in our likeness, and let them rule...be fruitful and increase in number; fill the earth and subdue it'. (Genesis 1:26,28)*

Before God formed Adam from the dust of the earth he spoke a specific word **about** the purpose and destiny of all mankind, including us. After he had formed Adam and Eve God then spoke that same word **to** them. It was important that they heard it. They grew used to hearing God's voice, and they were expected to live by it. The word that God spoke **about** mankind and **to** Adam was a creative word that has never been revoked; God has never taken that word back. It is still there, being fulfilled.

God's unchanging purpose is to fill this whole earth with a people in his image, a people like his Son Jesus. Even the sin and fall of Adam and Eve has no effect on this word; it has been spoken by God, and is still effective and being worked out today by God through his people. **Therefore, every word God speaks to us is**

always in line and accord with this very first word he spoke about and to mankind.

This truth is absolutely vital for you to grasp in living the *Circle of Life*. God speaks to us about many things: how to be good husbands, wives, fathers, mothers and children. He tells us how we should behave as employers and employees; how to care for the poor; how to handle money. He commands us to be baptised in water and in the Holy Spirit; we need to belong to a church that is worthy of God. God tells us the truth about ourselves, who we are in Christ, that all our sins have been forgiven and we are brand new creations. All these things that God speaks to us about are the outworking of that original word he spoke when he brought mankind into being. I can't stress this point too much. You have to grasp it and get it into you; you have to hear it and allow it to soak right down into your heart. It has to become part of you.

We are going to learn that all our speaking must be in the same vein as God. Our words have creative power too. Our destiny is to fulfil what God spoke to Adam and Eve in the first place, because he spoke it to us too.

Now, if you have not grasped the incredible truth of what you have just read, don't go any further right now. Please read these paragraphs again and ask the Holy Spirit to reveal to you the power and the reality of this truth. Hear God speak to you and get it into your heart. It will change your life.

The most important words we can hear, indeed the words we must train ourselves to hear, to receive them into our hearts so we can become them, are the words that God speaks. Jesus said that we live *'by every word that comes out of the mouth of God'* (Matthew 4:4). Therefore, we have to know the various ways in which God speaks to us.

How does God speak to us?

God speaks through the Bible: the Word of God

First and foremost God speaks to us through his Word, the Bible:

All scripture is God breathed, and is useful for teaching, rebuking, correcting and training in righteousness, so that the man of God may be thoroughly equipped for every good work. (2Timothy 3:16-17)

The Bible is the Word of God. It was breathed out by him, spoken from within his very being. During a period of 1,500 years he breathed out through the Holy Spirit, so that the human authors of the Bible produced a completely reliable and trustworthy book. The Bible is God's inspired, infallible and inerrant complete communication to us. God will speak to you every time you read it. Therefore, whenever you open it approach it with excitement, anticipation and expectation. The Holy Spirit within you is the same Holy Spirit who inspired the writers. He will help you and speak to you as you read these amazingly powerful words. Come to it with faith, asking God to show you the truth of the Word. Read it every day; and as you read hear what God is speaking to you.

Everything God speaks to you will always be in complete accord and agreement with the Bible. God will never ask you to do anything contrary to his Word; it is impossible for him to do so. If you hear a voice telling you to go on a mission trip to Mars to preach to all the left handed vegetarians there, you can guarantee it's not the voice of God! He is so identified with his Word that if God ever acted against it he would cease to exist, which is completely impossible:

I will praise you, O LORD…for you have exalted above all things your name and your word. (Psalm 138:1-2)

The Word of God is his integrity, and he is behind all his Word. It never even enters his mind to act contrary to his Word. Therefore you can trust it. Later on, when we discuss the importance of having a believing faith this wonderful truth will become even clearer for you.

God speaks through Jesus: the Word of God

In the beginning was the Word, and the Word was with God and the Word was God. (John 1:1)

> *The Word became flesh [was made incarnate] and dwelt among us. (John 1:14)*

God speaks to us through his Son, the Lord Jesus Christ, who is the incarnate Word of God. He is God's ultimate communication to us. Hebrews 1:2 tells us that God '*has spoken to us by his Son.*' The Bible and Jesus are closely related; there is no other Jesus except the one revealed in the Word of God; and the Word of God can only be properly understood through a living relationship with Jesus by the Holy Spirit, who breathed the Word from God through inspired men. Jesus is not the Bible; he is greater than the Bible, because he is God. We do not worship the Bible; we worship Jesus, the God of the Bible. Nevertheless the Bible is the only means by which we meet Jesus. The 'Jesus' of the Koran and the 'Jesus' of the Book of Mormon do not exist. There is only one true Jesus, and that is the Jesus of the Bible. He is God the Son.

My grandmother, a very simple woman from a small English village, knew more about the power of the Bible than some professors of theology with their vast knowledge of all the biblical languages and their academic degrees. Why? She knew the Jesus of the Word. If they don't know Jesus then they are the most ignorant of men and know nothing of the Word of God. That's just the way it is. I'm not anti-academic: I have a PhD and a Masters degree in theology. But reading and studying the written Word of God without a relationship with the incarnate Word of God won't help you.

God speaks through preaching & teaching

God also speaks to us through the preaching and teaching of the Word. That's why you must make sure you're in a church where the Word of God is believed, taught and lived by. Avoid preachers who want to fill you with their own latest opinions, or with the worldly views of the age. Just because a preacher comes on TV with a Bible or stands in a pulpit does not mean he is right. Does he preach and teach the Word of God? To whom he is accountable? Is he a one man show? Or is he part of a wider body of ministers to whom he is answerable?

If you're in a church where the leaders don't believe the Bible is the Word of God or they deny that Jesus is God, get out as quickly as you can and get into a church where you can hear some truth. Your life is at stake.

God speaks through prophecy & other spiritual gifts

God has given many spiritual gifts to his church (see 1Corinthians 12 and Romans 12). He speaks to us through these gifts of the Spirit. Prophecy is the one gift we are all urged to covet (1Corinthians 14:1). I appreciate belonging to a church where prophecy is regularly practised with all the practical instructions and safeguards the Word of God gives us for its use. Every true prophecy will be in line with the Word of God, and will *'strengthen, encourage and comfort'* the people of God (1Corinthians 14:3). It will never replace the Word of God; but it will build up the church when used properly. If you've never prophesied, or it's been a while since you did, stir yourself to do it. It will help you in your hearing, because before you prophesy you have to hear what God wants to say to his people.

God speaks through the creation

When God wanted to show Abraham the greatness of his plan for him, that he was going to have a son,

> *God took him outside and said, "Look up at the heavens and count the stars – if indeed you can count them." Then he said to him, "So shall your offspring be." (Genesis 15:5)*

King David looked up at the hills around him and asked:

> *Where does my help come from? My help comes from the LORD, who made the heavens and the earth. (Psalm 121:1-2)*

As Abraham gazed at the stars in the sky and David stared at the hills, God spoke to them about his greatness and incomparable power and ability to keep his word. It helped build their faith. God will do that for you too: whenever you see a rainbow it's a reminder of God's covenant faithfulness (Genesis 9:16). When you see the grass growing in your garden, remember that God will always make sure you have clothes to wear (Matthew 6:30). Every time you hear a bird sing or see one feeding, remember that the same heavenly Father who is providing that worm will feed you – with something far nicer than worms! (Matthew 6:26)

God speaks through our leaders & the Body of Christ

God speaks through our church leaders and our brothers and sisters in the Body of Christ. Our leaders have been placed by God in their positions of responsibility to 'keep watch over our souls' (Hebrews 13:17). The Bible knows nothing of the independent, individualistic Christian who hops from church to church with no sense of accountability to those over them in the Lord. In fact, the New Testament emphasises the very opposite: we are born again into a community, the church, the Body of Christ. Here we have privileges and responsibilities; we admonish, encourage and care for one another (Colossians 1:28; 3:16; 1Thessalonians 5:12).

Nearly all the New Testament epistles were written to communities, to people living a common life in the fellowship of the Holy Spirit, who were expected to take responsibility for one another. It doesn't mean that my Christian friends live my life for me; I am responsible for my own life and actions. I have to hear God for myself. Nevertheless, I expect to hear God speak to me through the words of my brothers and sisters. Sometimes I have major decisions to make and I need the wisdom of my leaders and valued friends. As a leader I sometimes have to hear from God for the sheep of my flock: when they need wisdom or are facing a situation where they need to be sure that they are hearing the Spirit clearly. Too many Christians make life changing decisions totally independent of any input from wise leaders, but

> *The wisdom that comes from above is...submissive [open to reason]. (James 3:17)*

A few years ago I was visiting Christians in a certain country. It was a particularly hazardous trip because the authorities were persecuting believers at the time. If my colleagues and I were caught we would have been in big trouble, and so would the Christians we were visiting. Just before I flew to that country I had a telephone call from a lady. This lady hears from God, but she was quite nervous on the phone with me. She did not know that I was on my way to a dangerous situation, but that day as she was sitting in her kitchen I came to her mind. She felt the Holy Spirit prompt her to call me and to say to me 'everything will be alright.' That's all she had to say to me. She felt rather stupid calling me with such a simple phrase, but the Holy Spirit impressed on her even stronger to call me. Eventually she picked up the phone and rang. When she told me these words I rejoiced: God had spoken to her to speak to me! I would be OK.

Towards the end of our trip my friends and I were apprehended by the authorities. Immediately the words God had spoken to me through this lady came to me: 'Everything will be alright.' I spoke them back to the Lord as his promise to me and my companions; thirty minutes after being detained we were released — with the profuse apologies of the commanding officer ringing in our ears! God is a God who speaks.

The church is the *'family of believers'* (Galatians 6:10). The King James Version translates that verse as 'the household of faith'. We are a people who build each other up in faith. We will devote some chapters to how we practically do that.

God speaks through anything!

There's no way of getting around this one: God is able to speak to us through anything:

- A donkey: Numbers 22:30
- A pagan king: Daniel 4:34-35
- Fire from heaven: 1Kings 18:36-39
- A finger writing on a wall: Daniel 5:5-26

In all these ways of speaking God shows us that we must never restrict him in a straitjacket or put him in the box of our own limitations. He is God and will not be defined nor confined by us. He can speak to us in any way he chooses. He has spoken to me while I have been listening to classical music and reading biographies of political leaders. I have heard his voice as I listened to an interview with a famous football manager. God spoke to a friend of mine to move from the USA to Wales. At the same time he had an invite to go to Hawaii. Wales or Hawaii? He knew God wanted him in Wales; but the attraction of Hawaii was real. One day, as he was in his study he came across a cartoon of a Hawaiian surfer, holding his surfboard. The top of the board had been chewed off by a shark. God spoke to my friend: 'You can go to Hawaii if you want.' He came to Wales — very quickly! Don't limit the ways in which the Holy Spirit can communicate with you.

We constantly need to hear God speak, and we must expect to hear his voice at any time.

God speaks through the Holy Spirit

All the ways that God speaks mentioned here depend on this last point: God speaks to us through the Holy Spirit, who has come to live within us if we are Christians. When we receive Jesus as Lord he comes to live in us in the Person of the Holy Spirit (Romans 8:11). He is the One who brings me into a relationship with God as my Father (Romans 8:14-16). It's only through the Holy Spirit that I know Jesus (John 14:15-18). It's the Holy Spirit who speaks the Word of God to me and I have to learn to listen to that voice. Jesus said of the Holy Spirit:

> *When he, the Spirit of truth comes, he will guide you into all truth. He will not speak on his own; he will speak only what he hears, and he will tell you what is yet to come. He will bring glory to me by taking from what is mine and making it known to you. (John 16:13-14)*

Since the Holy Spirit hears what God has to say, his role is to tell me what God has to say to me. And my role is to train myself to listen to the voice of the Spirit. In doing so I hear the voice of God.

Of course, in order for me to hear God in this way I have had to learn to be at home in hearing him first and foremost through the Word of God. This is where the Holy Spirit has schooled and trained me for a long time: I have learnt to soak myself in the Word of God, to listen to the Holy Spirit as I read, and to ask him questions as I meditate on it. Reading the Bible is never a chore or a drudge for me. Whenever I open its pages I meet the God who has the words of life, who is willing and ready to speak to me, who has created and designed me to hear and obey that voice. Therefore I read the Word of God every day; in the same way I have to eat my natural food I have to eat my Spiritual food. If you really want to hear God's voice then you will have to cultivate a relationship with his Word. There is no other way.

God is a speaking God; he has something to say on everything. He is a real chatterbox, but he never wastes a word. His word is creative; it is life-forming and life-sustaining. It has the same power as the word which brought the universe into being. God speaks to you all the time. Are you listening to him? Or do you listen to the voice that we'll look at next? That's a completely different voice — the voice of the devil.

CHAPTER FOUR

The Liar

Did God really say? (Genesis 3:1)

Let's get something straight right at the beginning: the devil is a liar, a deceiver, a stranger to the truth, and an accuser. He hates God and he doesn't like you. Jesus exposed the devil for who he really is:

> *He was a murderer from the beginning, not holding to the truth, for there is no truth in him.* ***When he lies, he speaks his native language****, for he is a liar and the father of lies. (John 8:44)*

Jesus tells us the truth about the biggest liar of all time. Satan is the originator and instigator of every lie ever told. He is behind every piece of gossip. He is the master deceiver. Every time he opens his mouth he has one aim: to destroy the character of God and make you ineffective as a child of God. Sadly, far too often, he is very good at what he does.

The voice of the Devil

We saw in Genesis 1 how creative and full of life the voice of God is. Now turn over to Genesis 3 and, in total contrast, we'll see the very first occasion that the devil speaks:

*Now the serpent was more crafty than any of the wild animals the LORD God had made. He said to the woman, "**Did God really say**, 'You must not eat from any tree in the garden'?" (Genesis 3:1)*

Do you see the devil's crafty, devious tactic? First of all he didn't come to Adam, the head of the human race; he came to Eve, his wife. That is not a sexist remark: headship is a major principle in the Godhead and in his creation. The devil seeks to usurp it at every opportunity. Then he slyly approached Eve with a question, not an all out onslaught, just a suggestion, an innocent remark, a conversation opener. He asked her a question, but in it he questioned the words of God. In doing so he began his assault on the very trustworthiness of God. He was attacking the character, the integrity, the very nature of God: 'Did God **really** say?' 'Can you really trust what God said? Can you trust him at all?'

God is a faithful God:

He is the Rock, his works are perfect, and all his ways are just. A faithful God who does no wrong, upright and just is he. (Deuteronomy 32:4)

The faithfulness of God is the ground of our trust in him. If you question somebody's faithfulness, then you no longer trust them. If Satan could remove Eve's trust in the integrity of God he could separate God from his creation.

On the surface Eve did well. But look closer at the story. To begin with, she should never have listened to him in the first place. But she got into a conversation with the devil. Far too many Christians spend more time talking about or to the devil than God. They are frightened of him, and talk as if he's on their back rather than under their feet. Notice what Eve said to the devil:

The woman said to the serpent, "We may eat fruit from the trees in the garden, but God did say, 'You must not eat fruit

> *from the tree that is in the middle of the garden, and you must not touch it, or you will die.'" (Genesis 3:2-3)*

Check her words carefully; there's something wrong there. Can you spot it? God had not actually said what she claimed he had. God had actually said,

> *'You must not eat from the tree of the knowledge of good and evil, for when you eat of it you will surely die.' (Genesis 2:17)*

God never mentioned touching the tree; his command was not to eat from it. You might think that's not a big thing, just a minor detail. No, no, no. Somewhere in the process of hearing Eve had failed to listen in her heart to what God actually said; now she was vulnerable to the devil's ploy. He had her in his grasp. Immediately he went for the kill:

> *'You will not surely die,' the serpent said to the woman. 'For God knows that when you eat of it your eyes will be opened, and you will be like God, knowing good and evil.' (Genesis 3:4-5)*

Here is the outright lie. Satan told Eve that she and Adam would become like God if she believed him and ate the fruit of the tree. But Adam and Eve *were* already like God — they had been made in his image (Genesis 1:26-28). But now they were doomed — and so were we — because they listened to the voice of the accuser and chose to believe him rather than God. We know Adam was present while all this was going on: Genesis 3:6 tells us he was standing next to Eve while the serpent was speaking his evil words.

Once the devil had trapped Adam and Eve the die was cast. He had blatantly called God a liar, and had not been stopped by people who knew better. Isn't that ironic? The father of lies accusing the Father of truth of lying! Satan's tactics are still the same: 'God let you down; he doesn't really love you; he'll never forgive you for that sin.' If you have ever heard those words, either audibly or as a thought in your mind, guess who was speaking to you? That's right: the old liar. Don't listen to him; he's only going to cause trouble and destruction.

Satan's mission

Satan's sole aim is to destroy the character of God and frustrate God's eternal purpose (which includes the devil's own eternity in hell). One day he is going to be cast into a lake of fire (Revelation 20:10), and he is doing everything he can to prevent or delay that day. He's not stupid.

Therefore, just as every word that God speaks to us is in line with the very first word he spoke about and to us in Genesis 1:26-29; so **every word that the devil speaks is aimed at preventing the fulfilment of these verses in the Word of God**.

We have to understand that the devil is not ultimately interested in us, he's after our Father. We are the pinnacle of the creation, unlike any other species on the face of the earth, the apple of God's eye, created in his image. As Christians we are new creations in Christ, and

> *You were taught, with regard to your former way of life, to put off your old self, which is being corrupted by its deceitful desires; to be made new in the attitude of your minds; and to put on the new self,* ***created to be like God in true righteousness and holiness****. (Ephesians 4:22-24)*

We are the battleground for the devil, because we are the Body of Christ, the church. We are the instruments of the Kingdom of God, establishing his rule on the earth. At the Cross Jesus demolished Satan's power, '*destroying the works of the evil one*' (1John 3:8). But if he can get to us and make us live in such a way that diminishes our effectiveness as children of God, he thinks he can get to God. So what does he do? He understands the power of words; he witnessed the creation of the physical universe. He was part of the heavenly host that sang for joy when they witnessed God calling into being this wonderful planet earth (Job 38:7). He saw his own words wreak havoc and destruction as Adam and Eve believed him and acted on his words. He was driven from the presence of God when he rebelled and felt the power of the curse as God made him that awful promise: *'The Seed of the woman will crush your head'* (Genesis 3:15). So he tells us lies to get us to believe him rather than God. The tragedy is that millions of Christians allow him to manipulate them. The ultimate deception is to believe a lie is the truth.

Satan targets Jesus

Satan even tried this tactic with Jesus. At the beginning of Jesus' public ministry, at his baptism, God the Father spoke from heaven in an audible voice:

> *'This is my Son, whom I love; with him I am well pleased' (Matthew 3:17).*

What did Satan do? At the earliest opportunity, when Jesus was in the desert, hungry after a forty day fast, he spoke to him. Notice very carefully the very first thing he said in addressing him:

> *'**If** you are the Son of God, tell these stones to become bread.' (Matthew 4:3)*

This is exactly the same method the devil had successfully used with Eve. But this time he was up against a far more formidable foe. Jesus replied,

> *'It is written; man does not live on bread alone but by every word that comes out of the mouth of God' (Matthew 4:1-4).*

Two more times the devil tried it; each time Jesus withstood him. Listen; please hear what God is speaking to you right now: if Satan tried this tactic with Jesus, you can guarantee he'll try it with you. He'll speak suggestively to you, lie through his teeth to you, and assail you with innuendo and falsehoods, just to get you to believe him rather than God. His is the other voice, and you have to recognise it for what it is. Sometimes it will be subtle; other times it will be all out attack. But you have to realise what it is: the lies of an enemy.

Just the other day I was talking to a Christian friend who had recently been going through a major challenge. They woke up one Sunday morning and for the first time ever began to wonder whether they should join their brothers and sisters at the meeting that day. This person has loved the Lord for many years and has been a fantastic servant to God and his people. But in the past months they had been tempted to walk away by the lure of a relationship with a non Christian of the opposite sex, who had been expressing an interest in them (my friend is not married). After much struggling, my friend decided to go to the meeting. At the end the preacher just happened to pray a prayer concerning this very issue that cut into the heart of my friend. They realised that the enemy had been trying to seduce them away by words spoken to them. All the while during this period another voice had also been speaking: the voice of God. Happily my friend recognised what was going on; they told me afterwards it was being able to discern between the two voices that saved them.

As a new creation in Christ you are designed to listen to the voice of the Spirit of God within you. It's natural for you to live like that. As you spend time in God's Word, as you pray, fellowship with people of the Spirit, fellowship the Spirit himself, and speak in tongues, then you will get used to hearing the voice of God. Sometimes people ask me how I recognise it. At home the phone will sometimes ring and when I answer it the voice at the other end just says *'Hi.'* I know that voice just by the tone, the sound, the pitch, the word. It's my wife, Dianne. We have been married nearly thirty years; her voice is the most familiar human voice I know. I can even pick it out in crowded room. How? Over the years it has become part of me; I just know it.

The voice of the devil grates on me. It's like fingernails being scratched on a blackboard.

Which of the two voices do you listen to? The one that has your attention and controls you is the one you believe. It's the one you trust because you have faith in it.

CHAPTER FIVE

Believing Believers

The righteous will live by faith. (Romans 1:17)

Faith comes from hearing, and once we have heard, we have to move to the next part of the *Circle of Life*: believing. We actually put our faith in those words of life which God is speaking to us. We have already established that two voices are continually speaking to us. Please don't think, however, that God is on one shoulder and the devil is on the other, that both of them are whispering in your ear. The Holy Spirit took up residence within you when you received Jesus Christ as Lord: *'the Spirit of him who raised Jesus from the dead is living in you'* (Romans 8:11), and you are designed to hear him. Whenever you hear him the next step you have to take is to believe what he speaks to you.

'I don't have any faith'

A Christian should never say they have no faith. They may not have sufficient faith; indeed, we all should be aiming to grow in faith. Our faith is always increasing; nevertheless **every** believer in Christ has faith. The Bible tells us that we become Christians by putting our faith in Jesus to save us from our sins and make us right with God:

> *If you confess with your mouth, 'Jesus is Lord,' and* ***believe*** *in your heart that God raised him from the dead, you will*

> *be saved. For it is with your heart that you* ***believe*** *and are justified, and it is with your mouth that you confess and are saved. As the Scripture says, 'Anyone who* ***trusts*** *in him will never be put to shame.' (Romans 10:9-11)*

The best known verse in the entire Bible simply says:

> *For God so loved the world that he gave his only begotten Son, that whoever* ***believes*** *[has faith, puts their trust] in him will not perish but have everlasting life. (John 3:16)*

Faith is actually a free gift from God; he is so good and gracious that in the moment we repent of our sins and turn to him for salvation he enables us to have faith:

> *For it is by grace you have been saved, through* ***faith***—*and this not from yourselves, it is the gift of God. (Ephesians 2:8)*

If you are a Christian then you are a believer; you have faith. In fact, the early Christians in the book of Acts called themselves 'believers' (Acts 1:15; 2:44; 4:32; 5:12; 9:41). It was not until many years later that the title 'Christian' came into being (Acts 11:26). A Christian is a believer, one who lives by faith in Jesus Christ. When you became a Christian you believed something that you heard: that Jesus Christ died for your sins and rose again from the dead as your Lord and Saviour. You knew he was alive but you didn't see him in the flesh. You had faith that if you asked him into your life he would come in. You entered the Kingdom of God by faith, but you didn't actually see Jesus with your physical eyes that day. Your faith worked, and you have that faith now.

We don't just *become* Christians by faith, however: we *live* as Christians by faith. We have to adopt, therefore, the lifestyle of believing: we are believing believers. Always remember that for you faith is as natural as breathing.

Hearing & Believing

Since faith comes by hearing words (Romans 10:17), it is in believing those words that faith is established, increases and ultimately acts. Each word we hear has the power to create faith. This is a really important aspect of faith and is one where many Christians struggle. They say they have faith, they say they are trusting God, but too often they are like the man with the demonised son who Jesus met. The man cried out to Jesus:

> *If you can do anything, take pity on us and help us. 'If you can?' said Jesus. 'Everything is possible for him who believes.' Immediately the boy's father exclaimed, I do believe; help me overcome my unbelief!' (Mark 9:23-24)*

This man was struggling with doubts. His son had been possessed by an evil spirit for many years. He brought the boy to Jesus to heal him; therefore he must have already heard that Jesus had healed others who had the same condition as his son. But when he arrived Jesus was not there. So the disciples tried to cast out the evil spirit, but they couldn't do it. The father's faith was under attack as he saw his son still in the grip of this horrible spirit that was trying to destroy him. And as he waited for Jesus another voice began to speak to him, putting doubt in his mind. When Jesus finally turned up the man's opening retort to him was *'if you can.'* Jesus challenged him strongly on his words, because they revealed the depth and quality of his faith. Jesus could hear the voice of another in the man's question; he knew that the voice of the enemy had been at work. This was confirmed by the man's response: *'I have faith; help me overcome by non—faith, my doubts, my questioning whether you really can do this, that you really will do this. I believe that you can; I don't know if you will.'*

Sadly I meet this many times when I pray for the sick. These dear people read the Bible, hear the preaching of the Word and respond to an appeal, sometimes on several occasions. But they are still sick. They believe that God can heal them, but they don't know if he will. Some are no longer even sure whether God wants to heal them. Some of them have even been told by well meaning friends that their sickness is from God (I don't believe that). So when they come to me there is a general faith that God could do something but little or no expectation that the moment I lay my hands on them or speak the word of healing that anything will happen. They have a hope, but not the Bible kind of hope. So, before I lay hands on them I have to speak words of faith to them and get them to believe. Through helping people like this I see more people healed now than ever. There is nothing magical about me: I just believe the Word of God.

Compare this man who had the demonised son with the case of the Roman centurion whose servant was sick. He sent for Jesus to ask him to come and heal the servant, and Jesus agreed to go. However, the centurion then said something that quite amazed Jesus:

> *The centurion replied, "Lord, I do not deserve to have you come under my roof.* ***But just say the word, and my servant will be healed.*** *For I myself am a man under authority, with soldiers under me. I tell this one, 'Go,' and he goes; and that one, 'Come,' and he comes. I say to my servant, 'Do this,' and he does it." When Jesus heard this, he was astonished and said to those following him, "I tell you the truth, I have not found anyone in Israel with such great faith." (Matthew 8:7-10)*

This centurion had greater faith than anybody else in Israel at that time: more than the religious leaders, and more than Jesus' own disciples. He believed in the authority of Jesus' word. He didn't need any other evidence to prove the word was true; he didn't need the disappearance of a symptom before he had faith. The centurion didn't insist on a confirming sign to help him believe; he asked for nothing, because he had everything that was necessary for the miracle: he had the word. He just believed the word that Jesus spoke, and that word was sufficient. Having heard the word he believed it. The servant was healed. The centurion knew that behind the word that Jesus spoke to him was all the authority and ability of the God of heaven to perform that word. That's faith.

Let me give you one more example: it's vital we see the importance of believing and acting on the Word that is spoken to us without any other supporting physical proof. On another occasion a royal official from Capernaum came to Jesus when he was in Cana. He asked Jesus to come with him to heal his dying son. Notice what happened:

> *Jesus replied, 'You may go. Your son will live.'* ***The man took Jesus at his word and departed.*** *While he was still on the way, his servants met him with the news that his boy was living. When he inquired as to the time when his son got better, they said to him, 'The fever left him yesterday at the seventh hour.' Then the father realised that this was the exact time at which Jesus had said to him, 'Your son will live.' So he and all his household believed. (John 4:50-53)*

Jesus gave this person a very simple, uncomplicated word; it was easily understood and easy to act on. This was not rocket science: it didn't need an interpretation or deep explanation. All he had to do was believe; and the proof of his faith was to go home. Notice that in each of these stories Jesus refused to bow to the emotional pressures of the situation. He was not immune to the feelings of those involved: he felt for those who were pleading with him and for those who lay at death's door. Jesus was a man of compassion, but he also wanted people to rise above their adverse circumstances to a level where they lived by faith. He wants us to do the same. We have to be people who believe him, who take him at his word. God knows all your circumstances completely; nothing comes your way that takes him by surprise. He has your life in the palm of his hand and has something to say about everything in your life. Believe him.

The example of Abraham

Abraham is our father in the faith (Romans 4:11). All Christians are Abraham's seed or offspring because we are in Christ, **the** Seed of Abraham (Galatians 3:16; 26-29). The New Testament encourages us to follow his example in living by faith. Quite often I return to the story of Abraham in Genesis 12 to 25 to see how my father in the faith lived the *Circle of Life*. Let's draw out some things from his life that will help us see the link between hearing and believing.

We meet Abraham first of all at the end of Genesis 11. He was originally called Abram, which means 'exalted father.' He left Ur, near Babylon, with his father Terah and his wife Sarai, who was ten years younger than Abram. Significantly, the very first thing the Bible tells us about Sarai is that she was barren (Genesis 11:30). This young married couple expected to spend many years together, but with no expectation of ever experiencing the joy of raising children, and seeing their grandchildren. Such dreams weren't even a possibility; and in those days the stigma of barrenness was almost unbearable.

Some years later, after the death of Terah at a place called Haran, God spoke to Abram, who by now was seventy five years old:

> *"Leave your country, your people and your father's household and go to the land I will show you. I will make you into a great nation and I will bless you; I will make your name great, and you will be a blessing. I will bless those who bless you, and whoever curses you I will curse; and all peoples on earth will be blessed through you." So Abram left, as the LORD had told him. (Genesis 12:1-4)*

Hebrews 11:8 tells us more about this:

> *By faith Abraham, when called to go to a place he would later receive as his inheritance, obeyed and went, even though he did not know where he was going.*

It's true that Abraham didn't know where he was going, but he certainly knew what he was looking for:

> *He was looking forward to the city with foundations, whose architect and builder is God. (Hebrews 11:10)*

When God told Abram to leave Haran, he obeyed and went. Note that: he obeyed. Just put that one on the shelf for now; we'll come back to the aspect of obedience in another chapter. Abram left everything because God told him to. He heard the word of God and believed it. As the years went by God spoke to Abram again. He told him that he would give him children:

> *I will make your offspring like the dust of the earth. (Genesis 13:16)*

Imagine hearing those words you never dreamed you would hear: 'you will have children.' In spite of his experience, despite his situation, no matter that it was impossible, Abram believed what God told him. That's faith.

The big moment for Abram came a little later. No children had come and Abram concluded that God meant that one of Abram's servants would be his 'offspring'. But God had other ideas:

> *Then the word of the LORD came to him: "This man will not be your heir, but a son coming from your own body will be your heir." He took him outside and said, "Look up at the heavens and count the stars—if indeed you can count them." Then* ***he said*** *to him, "So shall your offspring be."* ***Abram believed the LORD****, and he credited it to him as righteousness. (Genesis 15:4-6)*

Here was a man now approaching his mid eighties, and God told him that he was going to be a father — of millions of children. Abram believed God: he heard the word and believed it, despite every natural circumstance and situation that militated against such a miracle. It was against all hope (Romans 4:18), but he chose to believe. Abram had faith in the word because he believed in the integrity and faithfulness of the God who had spoken the word.

Soon after, Abram became a father: Sarai his wife gave him her servant Hagar; she and Abram had a son called Ishmael. But still God had not finished with Abram.

Twenty four years after first speaking to him God spoke to Abram again, who by now was ninety nine. This time God changed Abram's name to 'Abraham', the 'father of many nations,' and changed Sarai's name to Sarah. Then God told Abraham something he never ever expected to hear:

> *'I will bless Sarah and will surely give you a son* **by her.** *I will bless her so that she will be the mother of nations; kings of peoples will come from her.' Abraham fell facedown; he laughed and said to himself, 'Will a son be born to a man a hundred years old? Will Sarah bear a child at the age of ninety?' God said, 'Your wife Sarah will bear you a son, and you will call him Isaac.' (Genesis 17:16-19)*

This was by far the biggest thing that Abraham and Sarah had ever had to believe God for. All their married life, which by now was many years, they had lived with the reality of her inability to have children. This had been compounded by the fact that she was now ninety years old and Abraham was almost one hundred. He had had a child at eighty six, but that was thirteen years ago. Now God was speaking to them about an utter impossibility. Why put them under such pressure? Why ask them to believe such a thing? Why bring up such a sensitive subject after all these years? Why play with their emotions in such a way? Why hadn't he spoken to them when they were younger? Well, that would have made no difference to the fact that Sarah was barren; now she was old and barren. But you know what? They both believed God:

> *By faith Abraham, even though he was past age—and Sarah herself was barren—was enabled to become a father because he considered him faithful who had made the promise. And so from this one man, and he as good as dead, came descendants as numerous as the stars in the sky and as countless as the sand on the seashore. (Hebrews 11:11-12)*

Some versions translate this passage: *By faith even Sarah, who was past age, was enabled to bear children because she considered him faithful who made the promise.*

How were Abraham and Sarah able to exercise such faith? **They considered him faithful who made the promise**. Romans 4:21 says a similar thing:

> *[Abraham was] fully persuaded that God had power to do what he had promised.*

That is the key to hearing and believing. Abraham believed the word of the Lord; he trusted what God spoke to him. He faced the facts of the situation head on: he was an old man and his wife was an old barren woman. Faith does not ask you to bury your head in the sand and ignore the circumstance. But he looked beyond the facts. Abraham had faith that the One who had the ability to speak all the stars into being and to hold them all in place was able to do what he promised Abraham. The word God spoke to Abraham was just as creative and powerful as the word God had spoken when he brought the universe into being. Behind the word that God spoke was God himself, with all his attributes. The Word of God is the most powerful, creative and reliable force in the universe. Isaac was born right on time.

God and his Word

This is vital for us when we come to believing: Who is making the promise to us? Is the person who is making the promise trustworthy? Are they telling the truth? Can they deliver on the promise? How can we be sure that they will do all they say they will? In a nutshell: is God trustworthy? We don't have faith in faith, we have faith in God. This is what Jesus said: *'have faith in God'* (Mark 11:22) Jesus urged us to have the God kind of faith.

Therefore, the most important question you ever face is: what is God like? That great man of God, AW Tozer said, 'What comes into our minds when we think about God is the most important thing about us.' Each one of us is the product of what we believe God to be like. We build our lives on our concept of God. You are the way you are at this point in life because you believe certain things about God. Let me explain. Some Christians read the Bible and 'hear' that God forgave them **all** their sins when they came to Christ:

When you were dead in your sins and in the uncircumcision of your sinful nature, God made you alive with Christ. He forgave us all our sins. (Colossians 2:13)

In spite of this wonderful reality, many years later they still live with their past life, which no longer exists, hanging around their neck like a lead weight. They say, 'I know the Bible says I am forgiven, but I don't feel forgiven; I still feel condemned.' These people don't believe. I'm not saying they're not Christians, I am saying they're not believing believers. In effect they say, 'I know the Bible says it but I don't really believe it.' They have a deficient understanding of God, because they don't trust what he says. He says, 'If you come to me and put your faith in Jesus to save you from your sins, I will forgive you of all your sins and make you into a brand new person.' They say, 'I don't feel it. If I felt it I would believe it.' God doesn't ask you to feel it then believe it: he says 'believe it.' Sadly such people find it difficult to trust not only God, but other Christians. The devil has trapped them in a web of lies.

Take God at his word

I am convinced that this aspect of the *Circle of Life* is one that the church desperately needs to recapture today: to be those who believe God and take him at his word. As Christians we say we believe in the Bible, that we believe it to be the Word of God. We have our doctrines about the Bible:

It is ***inspired***: it's breathed out by God. Even though it was written by men, they were the secondary authors. The primary author is God, who breathed his word through them on to the sacred pages.

It is ***infallible***: it does not deceive us but leads us into all truth. It never leads us into confusion or plays tricks with us. It never takes us up dead end streets or blind alleys. But it has to be handled correctly and treated properly. Each part must be read in the light of the whole, and the whole in the sum of all its parts.

It is ***inerrant***: it has neither error nor contradictions in it. It tells us the truth about God and ourselves. It records history one hundred percent accurately. It is right in what it says concerning issues such as marriage and sexuality. It is not a book which is confined to nor defined by the cultures it was written in: it is the eternal Book of God for every generation.

You might say, 'I agree with all these things.' Good. If you don't you need to come to a place of faith concerning the integrity and authority of the Bible. But even if you are at that place, the challenge is to believe **all** it says.

Believe the God of the Word

I hope that by now you have grasped that we don't just have faith in the Bible. We have faith in the God of the Bible. The Bible is trustworthy because it is the Word of the God who is the God of his word. So our ultimate trust is in the God of the Word.

One of the ways God describes himself in the Word of God is as *El Shaddai* (Genesis 17:1). It means two things: first it means the *God of the Mountains*, the one who is totally invincible and all conquering, the Almighty God. It also is linked to the word for the female breast, and portrays the image of a mother suckling her baby with all the life enhancing milk that baby needs to thrive and grow. The baby never worries whether there is enough milk; it just feeds and feeds. The mother has all the milk necessary to feed her baby; her life is in that milk. It empowers and nurtures the baby as it grows. *El Shaddai* is the Almighty, invincible, all powerful God who has all the resources within himself to meet all the needs of all his people all the time, and he never runs out of resource. He is the God who is more than enough!

Jesus described him as the *'how much more'* Father (Luke 11:11-13). He told us to approach this great God and to keep on asking, to keep on seeking, and to keep on knocking (Luke 11:9-10). If we do that in faith then our *'how much more'* Father will ensure that we will keep on finding, we will keep on having doors open to us and we will keep on receiving. Believe God.

It's all about you

There is one more thing I need to say about believing. The Bible is a book about God: I often call it the autobiography of God. It was written by him for us so that we can know him for who he is. But the Bible is about us too; we are all over its pages. Every time I read it

I find myself being mentioned. The Bible is not just **for** me — it's **about** me. Let me show you.

John 3:16 clearly states that whoever believes in Jesus will have everlasting life. Well, I am a 'whoever.' So it must mean me. It doesn't say, 'only those under sixteen' or 'just those over fifty five;' it makes no mention of whether you're a man or woman; you're not disqualified if you're bald or have had your appendix removed. It says, 'whoever.' That's me.

In John 14:12 Jesus declared: 'Whoever believes in me will do the things I have been doing; and even greater things!' It says nothing about healing evangelists (praise God for them); nothing about pastors with seminary training; nothing about how long you have to be a Christian before it applies. It doesn't even say you might get lucky one day and see somebody get healed. Jesus just said, 'whoever.' That's me. It's you too: yes, you.

I never read the Bible with any sense of nostalgia: it's all about me and I'm alive in the present. It works for me now. Whenever I read passages like these I choose to believe that God wrote it with me in mind. I see in 2Corinthians 5:17 that I am a brand new creation: I believe it. I am not a sinner anymore; I am a saint with the nature of Christ in me. Ephesians 2:10 tells me I am God's workmanship, a priceless work of art fashioned by the Genius who put the heavens in place. Malachi 3 tells me to bring the whole tithe into the storehouse and God will open up the windows of heaven and bless me. I believe it. Romans 8:1 declares that there's no condemnation to those who are in Christ: that's me. The Word of God is living and active (Hebrews 4:12) — in me.

See yourself in the Word of God: read it with an attitude of faith that it's not only God who is on the page — so are you.

You are about to discover that when you put faith in God and his word, things really begin to happen. Next, we're going to learn how to speak properly.

CHAPTER SIX

Get that mouth in gear

It is with your mouth that you confess and are saved. (Romans 10:10)

So far we have placed two aspects of living by faith – hearing and believing – into the *Circle of Life*, that lifestyle which is natural for every Christian to live. Faith comes by hearing, and we believe what we hear. The third element in the circle is just as important: learning to speak properly. The Bible calls it 'confession.' Look closely at the following verses:

> *If you* ***confess with your mouth****, "Jesus is Lord," and believe in your heart that God raised him from the dead, you will be saved. For it is with your heart that you believe and are justified, and* ***it is with your mouth that you confess and are saved****. (Romans 10:9-10)*

> ***Out of the overflow of the heart the mouth speaks****. The good man brings good things out of the good stored up in him, and the evil man brings evil things out of the evil stored up in him. But I tell you that men will have to give account on the day of judgment for every careless word they have spoken. For by your words you will be acquitted, and by your words you will be condemned. (Matthew 12:34-37)*

> *Whoever acknowledges [lit.* ***confesses****] me before men, I will also acknowledge [lit.* ***confess****] him before my Father in heaven. (Matthew 10:32)*

Did you realise that in order to be saved you had to say something? Raising your hand in a meeting, praying a silent prayer or signing a decision card did not save you. In order for you to become a Christian you had to do two things. Firstly you had to believe that Jesus died for your sins, that he rose from the dead and that he is your Lord. Secondly, that act of faith had to be accompanied by something else so you could be saved. It was necessary that for you to be rescued from the dominion of darkness and be born again into the Kingdom of God you had to say something. In accordance with Romans 10:9 you had to confess.

What is confession?

That word 'confess' doesn't mean the same as when we own up to something we have done wrong: 'Yes officer, I confess, it was me. I did it.' The word used in the Bible literally means:

> **To say the same as; to agree with; to speak the same words as; to speak with the same voice.**

What happened when you were born again? You heard the gospel and knew you had to respond, so you put your faith in Jesus to save you from your sins. At the same time you said something: you may have prayed it out loud or been asked to say certain words by the person who led you to Christ. You said, 'Jesus is Lord,' or you prayed in your own words to Jesus, repenting from your sins, acknowledging his Lordship and asking him to come into you life. Whatever the form of the words, you said that you were receiving Jesus Christ as your Lord and Saviour.

In that moment Jesus, who is in heaven at the right hand of God the Father, heard your words as you confessed him before men (Matthew 10:32). He turned to the Father and said, 'Father, Roger has confessed me as Lord. He has agreed with you, said the same as you, he has spoken with the same voice as you. I am now confessing him before you.' The Father said to Jesus, 'that's good enough for me: he's saved!'

You see, when you confessed Jesus as Lord you were agreeing with something already said about him: that he is Lord. Who is the one who has already said that? God the Father:

> *God exalted him to the highest place and gave him the name that is above every name, that at the name of Jesus every knee should bow, in heaven and on earth and under the earth, and every tongue confess that Jesus Christ is Lord, to the glory of God the Father. (Philippians 2:9-11)*

> *God has made this Jesus, whom you crucified, both Lord and Christ. (Acts 2:36)*

You agreed, said the same as, spoke the same words as God the Father concerning Jesus: you verbally agreed with him. That was the moment you were saved. We have already discovered the power of God's words: they are creative. There is, therefore, also creative power in **your** words. When you speak agreement with God your words have the same creative power as his. If you had never confessed with your mouth you could never have been saved; but in that moment when you confessed Jesus as your Lord, you were born again and a new creation came into being:

> *If anyone is in Christ he is a new creation. The old has gone, and the new has come. (2Corinthians 5:17)*

The Law of Establishment

All this happened because you believed in your heart and confessed with your mouth. You enacted a very important principle or law that God created: I call it the Law of Establishment. You can see it at work in the Word of God:

> *On the testimony of two or three witnesses a man shall be put to death, but no one shall be put to death on the testimony of only one witness. (Deuteronomy 17:6)*

One witness is not enough to convict a man accused of any crime or offence he may have committed. A matter must be established by the testimony of two or three witnesses. (Deuteronomy 19:15)

If your brother sins against you, go and show him his fault, just between the two of you. If he listens to you, you have won your brother over. But if he will not listen, take one or two others along, so that 'every matter may be established by the testimony of two or three witnesses.' (Matthew 18:15-16)

Do not entertain an accusation against an elder unless it is brought by two or three witnesses. (1Timothy 5:19)

The truth of a matter could only be established on the testimony or agreement of two or three witnesses. Once the two or three spoke agreement concerning that matter, the truth of it was established. It was regarded as a reality only when the two or three witnesses agreed, when they said the same as each other. The matter might well have been true, but it could not be established on the word of only one witness. The agreement of the two or three, however, established it as fact. This same principle works with us in confession when we agree with God. His word is never in doubt, and because God is One in Three, he is his own witness anyway. The Father, Son and Holy Spirit agree on everything: that is one of the reasons why God's word is so powerful and effective. He is one God in three Persons: the Trinity. When this one God speaks to himself the three Persons always agree:

*Then God said, "**Let us** make man in our image, in our likeness... So God created man in **his** own image, in the image of God **he** created him; male and female **he** created them. (Genesis 1:26-27)*

Nevertheless, when it comes to our confessions in our agreement with God, he is the first witness and everything he says is true. When we confess what he says, our words become the second witness and the truth of what God has said become a reality **for us**. My confession of Jesus as Lord doesn't make him Lord: he already is Lord. The difference is that my confession changes my relationship with him: I surrender to his Lordship. God is a reliable witness all on his own; and when I confess with him as the second witness the power of his word becomes a reality for me.

Whenever we confess the same as God our words will have the same power as his; in fact our words are his words through our lips. Once we take hold of this amazing truth we will realise just how responsible we must be in the way we speak. I am going to share with you in the following chapters some ways in which you can unlock the power of God through your words.

A lifestyle of confession

We enter this new life in Christ through hearing, believing and confessing. But that's only the beginning; confession is not a one off experience. A few chapters back we saw that words are powerful; each one has the power to create or destroy. We also found out that faith comes from hearing words. The words that affect us the most and determine much about the way we live will be those that come from our own mouths. In fact, we rise or sink to the level of our confession. Jesus said that our words are so important that on Judgement Day they will acquit or condemn us:

> *Out of the overflow of the heart the mouth speaks. The good man brings good things out of the good stored up in him, and the evil man brings evil things out of the evil stored up in him. But I tell you that men will have to give account on the day of judgment for every careless word they have spoken. For by your words you will be acquitted, and by your words you will be condemned. (Matthew 12:34-37)*

This passage of Scripture excites me every time I read it. Jesus said that whatever we hear and believe and gets down into our heart will eventually come out of our mouths: we speak what we hear and believe. What we really think and believe will come out of our mouths. One day God will call us to account not just for our actions but for our words, because our words determine so much about us. One day all humanity will stand before God at the final judgement. If we have confessed Jesus as Lord our names are written in the Lamb's Book of Life (Revelation 21:27) and we will pass to the next judgement that will be for all Christians: our heavenly reward (see 1Corinthians 3:11-15). There God will judge us for how we have lived as Christians, examining not only what we have done but also what we have said. The New Living Translation of Matthew 12:37 says, *'The words you speak now reflect your fate then.'* Why is God so concerned about our words? He knows that our tongues have the power of life and death in them (Proverbs 18:21) and that to a great extent our actions are the result of our words. The way we speak determines the way we act. Since our words determine our destiny and our inheritance, God takes them very seriously. So should we.

Think about the words that come out of your mouth, often in those 'unguarded' moments. You've just arrived home after a hard day's work; the traffic was really bad; it's hot. You're tired and need a quiet half hour. As you walk in the house there is war: the children are fighting and the living room is a mess. Something rises up from within you and you snap: 'You kids! Why did we ever have you? You are the worst children in the world! Sometimes I hate you. Why can't you just grow up and get out of my life?'

Where did such words come from? It's no use saying, 'I never meant to say that.' You said it, and Jesus said that out of the overflow of your heart your mouth speaks. You said it because deep down you believed it. What is more, you sowed those words into your children. If they received them into their hearts then one day out will come, 'dad hates me; he doesn't want me in his life.' Your words are driving your children away from you.

You're banging a nail into the wall when all of a sudden you miss and the hammer hits your thumb. What comes out of your mouth? Someone cuts in on you at the traffic lights. What's your reaction? The preacher declares, 'God is good!' Why do you remain silent?

The mouth will speak

Whatever is in your heart **will** come out of your mouth: Jesus said so. Your heart is the place where all that you have been hearing and believing takes root; it is the inner man, the real you, the centre of your being. Your heart is the seedbed of faith. All the things that you have been hearing from that voice you choose to listen to and believe come to rest and become what you are. Out of the overflow, the abundance of that heart, words will come. And those words reflect your future fate and your current spiritual health - or sickness.

Some time ago I was in our church meeting when a particular man came forward to prophesy. We had received a number of clear prophetic words that morning, so I asked him if his word would add anything to what had come. He said no it wouldn't, so I thanked him and asked him to return to his seat, which he did. A few days later he happened to be in our church building so I began to chat with him about the meeting and attempted to encourage him about hearing from God and being willing to prophesy. Suddenly his face darkened and he blurted out: 'When you wouldn't let me prophesy last Sunday I really hated you.' I was stunned. I took him aside, sat him down and began to talk to him about what had overflowed from his heart. He tried to deny saying it; then he said he didn't really mean it like that. But he did. It soon became clear this man had major issues of anger in his life that he had tried to hide; but God had exposed him through his words. Eventually, over a period of time, he learnt the principles of faith that I am showing you here, and is now a man of peace.

An ongoing process

We are beginning to see how the process of the *Circle of Life* works. Your mouth is fed by your heart, which is fed by what you hear. When you speak, the first person to hear what you say is you; your own voice feeds your own heart. And so it goes on. If bad things are going into you, bad things will come out of you. Whatever you listen to and believe in your heart will come out of your mouth. Either you are confessing — agreeing with God; or you are confessing — agreeing with the devil. It's very simple really.

There is a saying, 'silence is golden.' But for Christians silence is deadly. Sometimes our meetings can be like graveyards: the silence is a sign of death. Even your silence speaks; it tells me that something is wrong. It's actually un-natural to be a silent Christian. You became a Christian by speaking and you live the Christian life by speaking. I know there are times when we are silent in the awesome presence of the Lord, when even the sound of a breath seems sacrilegious: but that's a different thing altogether. If, on a day to day basis, you don't speak your faith then there is something wrong — a voice told you to be silent — and that voice was not the voice of God. By its very nature faith speaks:

> *It is written: "I believed; therefore I have spoken." With that same spirit of faith we also believe and therefore speak. (2Corinthians 4:13)*

I'm not saying we just chatter and chatter: far from it. Once we learn the power of confession we will choose our words much more carefully. Neither does it mean we have to shout at the top of our voices all the time. It's nothing to do with volume; it's all to do with the power of the words themselves and our faith in that power. You might have the gentlest voice, but if you learn these ways of speaking you will realise that the words which leave your lips have the power to do whatever God wants to achieve.

Your word is God's word

Our confession is powerful; in fact it is creative. Our words have the power of life and death (Proverbs 18:21); they actually have the power to bring things into being. This may appear strange, but it really makes sense if you think about it. When you agree with God in your confession, you are saying what God has already said. Therefore your words are just as potent as his. Consider these two passages:

> *Joshua pronounced this solemn oath: "Cursed before the LORD is the man who undertakes to rebuild this city, Jericho: "At the cost of his firstborn son he will he lay its foundations; at the cost of his youngest he will he set up its gates." (Joshua 6:26)*

> *In Ahab's time, Hiel of Bethel rebuilt Jericho. He laid its foundations at the cost of his firstborn son Abiram, and he*

set up its gates at the cost of his youngest son Segub, in accordance with the word of the LORD spoken by Joshua son of Nun. (1Kings 16:34)

After the battle of Jericho, Joshua spoke out a word that God had spoken to him. A long time later Joshua died and several hundred years passed by. When Hiel decided to rebuild Jericho, the very thing Joshua said would happen did happen. Why? God had spoken to him, Joshua agreed, he spoke it out, and it came to pass. Even though it was the voice of a man it was also the Word of God.

And what about Abraham? He was originally called Abram, which means 'exalted father.' But God changed his name to Abraham, which means 'father of many nations.' But he wasn't; at the time this happened he had just one son, Ishmael. God said to Abram, 'You call yourself what I've said you are - the father of many nations.' So that's what Abraham did; every time he spoke his name, every time Sarah called his name, he heard himself saying what God was saying about him: 'I am the father of many nations.' He agreed with what God had said and so became what God said.

Finally, don't forget Elijah, the man 'just like us' (James 5:17). He stood in the presence of God and God spoke to him. When Elijah came before Ahab he said,

As the LORD, the God of Israel, lives, whom I serve, there will be neither dew nor rain in the next few years ***except at my word.*** *" (1Kings 17:1)*

Just in case you're not yet convinced that you can speak the word of God, let me show you a verse in the New Testament which confirms that what I am telling you is the truth:

If anyone speaks, he should do it as one speaking the very words of God. (1Peter 4:11)

There is no doubt that every believer in Christ is a powerful weapon for good in the hands of God. He has enabled us to open our mouths and speak his very word. Such words in no way supplant nor replace the written Word of God – the Bible. Anybody who claims such a thing is speaking with that other voice we hate so much. But let's take hold of this fantastic truth: God has empowered all his children to hear him, believe him and speak his word to such an extent that when we speak he will act according to his word spoken through us.

Since the habit of confession is such a vital part of the *Circle of Life* we must give it a lot of attention. Therefore, in the following chapters I am going to give you some very practical examples of the way you can develop a life of confession. I guarantee that if you put them into practice and make them part of your everyday living your whole life will be dramatically changed for the better.

Psalm 45:1 says:

My tongue is the pen of a skilful writer.

I'm now going to show you how you can write your own bestseller.

CHAPTER SEVEN

The Attitude of Gratitude

Give thanks in all circumstances, for this is God's will for you in Christ Jesus. (1Thessalonians 5:18)

Enter his gates with thanksgiving and his courts with praise; give thanks to him and praise his name. (Psalm 100:4)

I like to think that I am a well mannered person. My parents taught me to say please and thank you, and my father used to say that manners make a man. In the first of our practical applications of confession we're going to learn some manners: how to say thank you to God. The Bible calls it 'giving thanks in all circumstances.' One of the biggest lessons we can learn in living the *Circle of Life* is to give God thanks in every circumstance that comes our way, whether good or bad.

What is a circumstance?

We tend to think that circumstances are the big things in life: a job interview; taking an examination; moving house; getting married. But a circumstance is anything that happens to us; we have hundreds of them during the course of each day.

My first circumstance today occurred about six-thirty this morning: I woke up. That was the very first thing that happened to me. As I came around from my sleep my thought processes started to kick in. It was morning, another new day and I was alive. The tasks of the day ahead quickly filled my mind. In that very first circumstance of my day I gave God thanks. I spoke out these words: 'Thank you Lord for the new day. Thank you I'm alive.' I didn't shout them out loud: Dianne was resting next to me. But I opened my mouth and started my day by giving God something: my thanks. It put the whole day in perspective: to begin with I was alive. For some people in this city there was no new day; they died last night and lie in the mortuary right now. But God in his grace had given me another day in which to serve him, and I thanked him for it. Don't take your life for granted: you're only ever one heartbeat away from eternity.

That's the way I have learnt to begin every new day. Not only do I give God thanks for the day, I thank him for the home I live in; my family; the clothes I am wearing; the food I eat for breakfast; even the warm water in the shower! I foster the attitude of gratitude at the commencement of each day. Then as I face all the other circumstances of the day I am already in the habit of giving God thanks: 'Thank you Lord that you will give me all I need to get through this difficult business meeting today.' 'Thank you Lord that little Freddy went off to school happy.' 'Thank you Lord the train was on time.' All these things are the daily circumstances that we meet. In each one we discipline ourselves to adopt the attitude of gratitude and give God thanks.

You might say, 'Roger, that means I'm going to be giving God thanks all the time for seemingly trivial things.' Well, yes you will be doing a lot of thanksgiving, but nothing is trivial. It's all training you to handle the big circumstances. It also helps you in the *Circle of Life* because you're hearing yourself speak words of faith and you believe what you hear. The seedbed of faith in your own heart is being watered by your own confessions.

In all circumstances

Note what the Word of God says: we give thanks **in** all circumstances, not **for** all circumstances. Sometimes bad things happen to Christians through no fault of their own; don't let anybody kid you otherwise. Jesus himself told us:

In this world you will have trouble. But take heart! I have overcome the world. (John 16:33)

I train myself to give God thanks in the good circumstances. Then, if bad things come my way I don't fall apart. I don't end up in deep depressions and long pity parties. I don't thank God **for** the bad circumstance; that is spiritual masochism. But as I face a bad or difficult circumstance and go through it I have the same attitude of gratitude that flows out of me in the good times. The word 'give thanks' literally means *'to show gratitude, to be thankful, to give thanks.'* It means that we have to open our mouths and speak thanks. We express our gratitude to God in any and every circumstance, no matter what we are going through. We adopt an attitude of gratitude in everything. As I'll show you later, this actually saved my life on one occasion.

For some strange and incomprehensible reason this is really hard for some Christians; but the Bible is very clear. This theme of giving God thanks runs right through the Word of God. If you just spend a few minutes reading the Psalms you will be amazed at the number of times we are exhorted to constantly praise the Lord:

I will bless the LORD at all times; his praise will continually be on my lips. (Psalms 34:1)

I particularly love that verse in Psalm 100: *'enter his gates with thanksgiving and his courts with praise.'* Thanksgiving is the language of praise.

Let me say it again: we don't just **say** thanks; we **give** thanks. Something comes from within our inner man when we give thanks. It is an offering of worship. It's all about our attitude. We can say thank you with our mouths but in our hearts have an attitude of clenching our teeth and hissing, 'thanks very much, thanks for nothing.' That will get us nowhere in God. (It will get us somewhere, but not where we should be). No, we are meant to give thanks; when we do that we are giving God something of ourselves. We are really grateful; so we speak thanks to him in gratitude.

No matter what the circumstance, give God thanks: in sickness; losing a job; the death of a loved one; a car accident; a pay rise; the birth of a child; the banana you had for breakfast. Whatever happens to you, keep thanking God.

How to respond

If I lose my job I don't come to God to moan, neither do I act stupidly and thank God for making me unemployed. No, I come to him and say, *'Lord, I lost my job. I loved that job and it paid well. Even though I've lost it I want to thank you that you are a good God and you are the source of my life and my wealth. I thank you that I will not starve. I thank you for the resource of that job. Now it's gone another resource will spring up. I thank you that you are still the source of everything. I thank you that you will provide me with another resource. I thank you that the righteous are never forsaken and their children never beg bread (Psalm 37:25). I thank you we will have food and clothes for the children; we will not starve. I thank you that as I seek another job you will bless me because I am a tither and a sower and a giver. I am sowing to you now in giving my thanks and you will bless me so I can continue to be a blessing. You will open the windows of heaven and pour out such a blessing on me that I will not be able to contain it. You are a good God and I will praise you! Amen!!'*

This works - I have done it. Praise and thanksgiving is the language of faith. Therefore, you won't find me moaning, muttering, grumbling or gossiping. I won't keep silent when I need to be giving thanks. I have adopted the habit of giving thanks to God in every circumstance; and remember that circumstances are not just the big things in life - it's what happens to you all the time.

I thank him that I can walk, see, speak, and eat. I thank him for my clothes and the money in my pocket; for the car, for my family. Whatever happens to me I thank him that he is a good God. Since I began to do this my whole attitude towards life has changed.

This came into sharp relief for me again just recently. I was driving home with a friend who was staying with us. We were just talking together as we travelled along a road I go on every day, when BANG! — something hit my car. I pulled over to see that my wing mirror had been smashed by a car going the other way, and who had come too close to me. As I got out of the car I began to give God thanks — that nobody was hurt, that it was just the wing mirror, that I have a nice car in the first place. As I walked over to the other driver, whose fault it was, I was calm and composed. I maintained the attitude of gratitude. This continued the next day when I went to the garage to have the damage repaired. In what could have been a frustrating experience, I kept on giving thanks to God.

In *all* circumstances

Every circumstance you meet will have within it something you can give thanks to God for. Good circumstances seem easier than bad ones to discover that 'something.' The meeting of a financial need; a physical healing, or a successful job interview all provide you with all you need to express gratitude to your Father. But even when you're walking through the valley of the shadow of death you can still thank him: 'You are with me' (Psalm 23:4). The prophet Habakkuk discovered this:

> *Though the fig tree does not bud and there are no grapes on the vines, though the olive crop fails and the fields produce no food, though there are no sheep in the pen and no cattle in the stalls, yet I will rejoice in the LORD, I will be joyful in God my Saviour. (Habakkuk 3:17-18)*

Learning to give God thanks in all circumstances helps the confession of our faith. We hear ourselves constantly speaking good things to him. We give no opportunity for the enemy to get in and derail our faith, especially at those vulnerable times when things may not be going the way we planned. The more we do it, the more our hearts are filled with faith.

Try it for yourself

As you come to the end of this chapter, just take a moment to put what you have read into practice. Perhaps you are at the end of the day, about to go to bed. Maybe it's lunchtime and you're eating a sandwich. Or you could be sitting in the waiting room of the doctor or dentist. Wherever you are right now you will have gone through many circumstances already in your day. Why not begin to speak to the Lord and give him thanks? If you're going through a tough one, don't thank him **for** it; but thank him that **in** it he's still good. And when you've given him thanks just be quiet a moment and you'll hear him speak to you.

A Lifestyle

Giving thanks in all circumstances is a lifestyle I have learnt to live by. Possessing the attitude of gratitude has transformed me over the years. There's nothing special about me; those of you who know me are nodding your heads in agreement. If I can do it, anybody can do it. And since this principle of giving thanks in all circumstances is required of me by the Lord, then that's what I do. On Judgement Day, when I give account of my words and my actions, I want the Lord to say to me, 'Thank you for having Kingdom manners: you learned the power and value of giving thanks to me. Here's your reward.'

If you begin to put this principle of faith into practice, then your life will change for the better. If it works for me it will work for you, because the Word of God works. Try it.

CHAPTER EIGHT

Make a good confession

Christ Jesus...made the good confession. (1Timothy 6:13)

So far we have discovered that for Christians living by faith is as natural as breathing. As we begin to combine all the elements of the *Circle of Life* we begin to see just how easy it is for us to be people of faith. This is the way God has designed us to live.

We have discussed three aspects of the circle: hearing, believing and confessing. Since faith comes by hearing words (Romans 10:17), the words that come out of our own mouths are paramount. They determine much of our destiny and inheritance. Remember that we rise or sink to the level of our confession. Either we live the *Circle of Life* or sink in the spiral of death.

Now let's talk about another dimension of confession. It's one we see mentioned in the New Testament and it concerns Timothy and Jesus:

> *Fight the good fight of the faith. Take hold of the eternal life to which you were called when you made your good confession in the presence of many witnesses. In the sight of God, who gives life to everything, and of Christ Jesus, who while testifying before Pontius Pilate made the good confession, I charge you to keep this command without spot or blame until the appearing of our Lord Jesus Christ. (1Timothy 6:12-14)*

In this passage of scripture we find the apostle Paul encouraging Timothy, his son in the faith. (If you encourage people when they are strong it will help them remain strong and prevent them growing weak). While there is no doubt that Timothy was a man of God (Paul called him one) and that he became a major leader in the early church, he seemed to have a tendency to be a little timid sometimes. If you read 1 and 2 Timothy you will find that several times Paul encouraged Timothy to be strong in spirit and body. On this occasion Paul reminded him to be a man of good confession.

Paul may have been telling Timothy to recall his confession of faith at his baptism; or perhaps he was referring to this incident when Timothy was set into his ministry:

> *Do not neglect your gift, which was given you through a prophetic message when the body of elders laid their hands on you. (1Timothy 4:14)*

Timothy received prophetic words when hands were laid on him. He agreed with them as he heard them, and they became his. Paul reminded him to use that powerful confession in his good fight: the fight of faith. Later on we will see that one of the ways we can defeat our enemies is by speaking to them. Here Paul told Timothy to remember how Jesus made his good confession before Pontius Pilate. So we can learn this lesson of making good confessions from the Master himself.

Pilate, you're right!

The incident Paul referred to occurred in John's gospel, where Jesus was being questioned by Pilate:

> *Jesus said, "My kingdom is not of this world. If it were, my servants would fight to prevent my arrest by the Jews. But now my kingdom is from another place." "You are a king, then!" said Pilate.* ***Jesus answered, "You are right in saying I am a king.*** *In fact, for this reason I was born, and for this I came into the world, to testify to the truth. (John 18:36-37)*

Here is Jesus' good confession, his 'saying the same as.' Pilate made a statement that was true, even though he was a godless man and didn't even believe it himself. He was probably even acting in an arrogant and dismissive manner to this bruised and battered carpenter before him. But Pilate said Jesus was what the Word of God said he was. The Bible says that the Messiah would be a King, the King of Kings. It's a major theme of the Old Testament prophets. Pilate was saying what the Word of God said. So when these true words left his lips Jesus agreed with him. He could not and would not let the opportunity pass to make a good confession/agreement with the Word of God. He didn't remain silent; neither did he question or deny Pilate's words. He didn't nod his head in silent agreement or give Pilate a thumbs up.

Even though the natural situation appeared to contradict the fact of his kingship, out of Jesus' mouth came the overflow of his heart. He said, 'You're right, I am a king. I agree with you because that's what the Word of God says I am and I agree with it.' That was his good confession. Jesus agreed with Pilate because Pilate was only saying what the Old Testament had said about the Messiah: he would be King. If you really think about it, Jesus was actually agreeing with himself since he wrote the Word of God in the first place.

That is what Paul told Timothy to do: to speak his agreement with what the Word of God said about him. It was to be a vital part of his armoury in the fight of faith.

'I am Abraham'

We've already mentioned Abraham several times, but let's remind ourselves again about his walk of faith. God changed his name from Abram ('exalted father') to Abraham ('father of many nations'), even though he wasn't. He had just the one son — Ishmael — at the time. But from the moment God called him 'Abraham' he never called him 'Abram' again. Neither did Abraham: he called himself only what the Word of God called him — 'father of many nations.' That was his good confession. He refused to answer to any other name. Every time he spoke his own name he agreed with the Word of God, with what God said he was, even though the unseen had not yet become seen. Abraham had his evidence and his title deed: the Word of God. His confession brought his miracle.

Abraham was ninety nine when God changed his name. He lived for another seventy six years in the good of it, seeing miracle after miracle and blessing upon blessing.

Confess the Word of God

How can you apply this dimension of confession in a practical way? Learn to read the Bible in different ways. Sometimes you'll read it quietly, maybe reading some of the Old Testament stories or the book of Acts. At other times you'll meditate on certain verses, chewing them over and over until they become part of you. But you also need to learn to read it out loud and respond to it vocally. There are times when I read the Bible silently and there are other times when I read it out loud. A habit that I have adopted is to confess agreement with the Bible; it is God's word after all. He has spoken; never forget that the Bible is God's actual spoken word written down. It is his integrity. So when I confess it I agree with it and the power of agreement comes into effect. God and I are speaking agreement together. And to agree with what God says will ensure that I speak and live in truth, which sets me free and keeps me free.

As my voice speaks the Word of God I hear my own voice agreeing with what is written. I hear my own mouth declaring the truth of God's word; I believe what I am hearing through my own voice. I speak agreement and that feeds the seedbed of faith in my heart. There's a real power that is released when we speak the Bible out loud.

But I also do more. Let's say I'm reading the following passage:

> *If anyone is in Christ, he is a new creation; the old has gone, the new has come! (2Corinthians 5:17)*

If you are in a place where you can read that verse out loud, do so now. Now do it again. And again.

Did you grasp the power of it as your voice agreed with the Word of God? That's what I do. Then I say something like this: *'That is what I am. I am a new creation in Christ. The old Roger Aubrey is dead and gone, buried in baptism. The new Roger Aubrey is alive and well in Christ. Everything is new, everything is different. There is nothing of my old life left; it's all gone. I am a brand new creation who never existed before. Hallelujah! Thank you Lord!'*

Take a verse like Romans 8:1 and read it out loud a few times. Then speak something like, *'I am in Christ Jesus, therefore there is now no condemnation for me at all. I am set free from my old life; it's completely gone, I am a new creation. The devil can't condemn me for anything. All my old sinful nature is gone. I am a holy one, a saint. I am born again to a new life. I am forgiven of all my sins. Thank you Jesus!'* Maybe look in the mirror as you say it. Look yourself in the eye. Or hold the Bible up to heaven as you make your confession. However you do it, use the Word to build yourself up by confessing it to yourself.

When you read the Gospels and Acts and see Jesus and the disciples healing the sick or performing miracles, speak out, *'I can do that! I can heal the sick! Jesus said that I will do all the things he did and greater things because he has sent the Holy Spirit who now lives in me!'* Then go out and do it.

The traditional 'quiet time' takes on a new dimension. I agree you're not likely to do this when you're reading the Word of God on a plane or a bus, but there is a time and a place when it should become a habit for you in the *Circle of Life*. If you can get used to hearing your own voice relating with the Word of God in private then it will revolutionise the way you speak when you're in public. The world is waiting to hear you.

CHAPTER NINE

Speak to yourself

Why are you downcast, O my soul? Why so disturbed within me? Put your hope in God, for I will yet praise him, my Saviour and my God. (Psalms 42:5)

On the surface this next aspect of confession might seem a little strange, since it's something most of us are discouraged from doing.

In the natural those who speak to themselves are often considered insane. However, in the Kingdom of God the opposite is true: you are in danger of become spiritually insane if you **don't** speak to yourself. There is a time to pray, a time to confess the Word of God, and there is a time to speak to yourself. Let's take a look at this Psalm and find out why and how the psalmist spoke to himself.

Things ain't what they used to be

When you read this Psalm you discover a man in serious trouble. I would venture to say that he was in danger of experiencing a complete breakdown. We don't know the circumstances of how he ended up in this situation, but as we read the first four verses of Psalm 42 we certainly encounter a troubled soul.

He has a deep longing to meet with God, but is unable to do so. He knows that it's only God who can satisfy his need; only God, 'the living God' is able to quench his thirst for a life that is no longer full. In verse three the psalmist admits his almost depressive state:

'my tears have been my food day and night.' I have no appetite, I cannot stop crying, there seems to be no respite or remedy for my predicament.

His problem is compounded by those around him: 'Where is your God?' Here we go again: those human voices speaking the words of the enemy, sowing doubt and confusion to his heart. 'God has abandoned you; he has forsaken you; your life is over. There's no way back for you out of this hole.' He calls to mind the past, but this only increases his anguish: it used to be so different, so much better, so fulfilling. In former days he was right in the middle of the move of God, one of the leaders. Those were the glory days when his heart was filled with joy and his life meant something to God. But now it all seems to have passed him by. Whatever has happened to him makes him feel abandoned, useless, a complete and utter failure. The next words from his lips will determine his destiny: perhaps a voice was whispering, 'End it now.'

Soul, listen to me

Notice what the psalmist didn't do: he didn't pray. Now I'm not against praying, not at all. Praying will sharpen your spiritual sensitivity like nothing else. But he didn't pray until verse nine: then he really prayed. There is a time to pray and there comes a time when the praying is done and you have to act in another way. That is what this man did. He did what seems a strange thing; but in fact it saved his life. He spoke to himself:

> *Why are you downcast, O my soul? Why so disturbed within me? Put your hope in God, for I will yet praise him, my Saviour and my God. (Psalms 42:5)*

He spoke to his seedbed, to his inner man, to his heart. Somehow he refused to give up on life; he just would not let himself slip away into oblivion. From the depth of his being (he expressed it as *'deep calls to deep'* in verse seven) he heard the voice of God. Then that voice of God himself spoke through the man to the man's own heart. He knew that he had to take authority over his own mind, his feelings, his depression, his future. And as he spoke the Word of God to himself his heart began to respond in faith. His own words spoken to himself produced faith and life. He began to declare, 'I will praise him, my Saviour and my God.' He lifted himself up out of his situation by his own words to his own heart. Then he prayed, crying out to God for restoration.

Many commentators believe that Psalms 42 and 43 belong together. If you read on into Psalm 43 you will find that the man speaks of his future with faith:

> *Send forth your light and your truth, let them guide me; let them bring me to your holy mountain, to the place where you dwell. Then will I go to the altar of God, to God, my joy and my delight. I will praise you with the harp, O God, my God. (Psalm 43:3-4)*

From being on the precipice of breakdown and collapse, the psalmist finds faith and a future, all because he spoke to himself.

Feed yourself

Whenever I teach this aspect of confession it is often the hardest thing for people to do when we practise it. Sometimes they just collapse in laughter, feeling absolutely ridiculous. I suppose that's because it's something they are just not used to. It's like they meet themselves for the first time. But as we keep on doing it people begin to realise and then release the power that is in this discipline.

Even though I've emphasised the example from Psalm 42 about the man who was in crisis, this is also a habit you should get into in the good circumstances too. I must admit that when I began to do it I felt acutely embarrassed. But the more I did it the stronger I felt. I began to speak strongly to myself: *'Come on, Roger, snap out of it. Why are you moping around like this? Life is not over. God is good; he is for you. Stop feeling sorry for yourself. There is a hope and a future for you. The best is yet to be. Come on, get up, trust in God, he is for you, he will help you, you're a child of God. Grow up, stop being childish and immature. Be the man God says you are. Don't give in to this attack, don't let it destroy you. Come on soul, rise up and be strong!'*

I look in the mirror and say to myself, '*Roger, you are the apple of God's eye. Today you will overcome that difficulty, it will not defeat you. Get rid of that negative attitude and pull yourself together. Come on, head up, chin out. You're a child of God: behave like one.*'

If you try this and fail, don't worry. Keep persevering and you'll discover that it will become easier. You might say to me, 'Roger, aren't you just trying to make us feel good about ourselves?' Yes, that's exactly what I'm trying to do! Have a go at this; you will need to find a time and place when you can do it, so you don't embarrass yourself in front of others. If you're facing a situation like the Psalmist was, do what he did. Instead of mulling it over and over in your mind, getting more and more depressed, take a deep breath and speak what he did. Why not use his words? Watch what happens to you. Your faith will grow.

CHAPTER TEN

Speak to the mountain

> *I tell you the truth, if you have faith as small as a mustard seed, you can say to this mountain, 'Move from here to there' and it will move. Nothing will be impossible for you. (Matthew 17:20)*

I really hope that you are taking hold of the importance of confession. I trust you are increasingly aware of the effectiveness of the words that come out of your mouth, and have become more sensitive to the words you hear.

The next aspect of confession we are going to look at is what Jesus called 'speaking to the mountain.' He said if we have mustard seed faith, then nothing will be impossible for us. We can speak to mountains that oppose us and they will disappear.

What did Jesus mean?

The disciples had been struggling to cast a demon out of a young boy, to no avail (see Matthew 17:14-21). They were frustrated by their failure; but Jesus simply rebuked the demon and it came out of the boy straight away, and he was healed. The disciples asked Jesus why he could do it and they couldn't. His reply was stark: *'It's because you have littleness of faith.'* That term means 'scarcely', 'hardly', 'barely' any faith. The disciples had a poor quality of faith. Consequently the words they spoke when they commanded this demon had no effect. Jesus took the opportunity to address the wider crowd that had gathered around to witness what was going on. He called them an *'unbelieving generation'* (verse 17). Jesus was constantly dealing with a people of low quality faith; it was so mixed with misunderstanding, doubt and fear it had been rendered ineffective.

Then he gave the remedy. He said, *'You can do it. All you need is real, genuine faith, and it only has to be the size of a mustard seed.'* A mustard seed was the smallest of all seeds, but still a genuine seed. Within that tiny seed was the power and the potential to grow. In fact, the mustard seed grows to be a massive bush. Jesus said that if we have this genuine faith, even though it's just as small as that mustard seed, it can do massive things: it can even it can move a mountain! That is such an encouragement. Jesus tells us that as long as we have genuine faith, the kind of faith I have been outlining in these pages, nothing is impossible for us. Real faith will achieve mighty miracles; it will do the impossible. We don't have to store up great quantities of faith before we attempt to do anything. All we need is genuine, pure faith.

What is a mountain?

Jesus was not commanding us to make fools of ourselves and prove our faith by shouting at Mount Everest, Mount Fuji, or Mount Kilimanjaro, to see if we can get them to move. We are not meant to play faith games. He was saying that there is a way to deal with the 'mountains' that stand against us. The disciples' mountain was the demon that refused to leave the boy, and the boy's continuing condition. The mountain also was their growing frustration and doubt if they could do anything about it. This situation wasn't a mountain to them when they first took the demon on. It was a molehill. But that demon was going nowhere while their faith remained so poor. Perhaps they went into the situation full of zeal and energy, but after a lot of activity nothing had changed. What had originally been a small matter, just a little obstacle in the road, had now become a massive mountain.

A mountain is any apparently immovable object that is defying you, opposing you, defying you, standing in your way. It can be a long term and difficult situation such as a sickness. It might be the house you have been trying to sell for a year; it could be long term unemployment. It seems to stand tall above you, looming high and threatening. It shouts at you: 'I'm not moving!' Wherever you go it blocks your path; it casts a giant shadow over everything else you do. It dominates the skyline of your life. If you have one, it's the very thing you're thinking of at this moment.

Speak to the mountain

How do you respond to such 'mountains?' Jesus said you don't just pray about a mountain, or talk about it. **You have to speak to it**. You open your mouth and in faith you speak to it directly. You take it on face to face. You tell it to be gone, to be 'thrown into the sea.' There is no need to rant and rave at it, or shout at the top of your voice. It's not about volume; it's all about the power of the word that comes from your lips. You can be the most gentle of speakers, but when you address the mountain it quakes. Remember, whenever you confess you say what God says. He has already said something about that mountain: it cannot succeed against you. The word that had the power to bring the universe into being is the same word you speak to that mountain.

If you can grasp the power of your words when you have faith in God, then nothing can stand against you, because as we have seen in previous chapters, you are speaking the very word of God to that mountain. And you know what? The Bible says:

The hills melt like wax before the LORD (Psalm 97:5).

If you are facing a mountain in your life right now, something that just refuses to budge (not sin, you must repent of that): face it head on, take authority over it, speak to it, and command it to go. Just speak in faith. All you need is genuine, real mustard seed faith and the biggest obstacle will go. It has to, because Jesus said so. Don't say, 'Well I spoke to the mountain, but the house still hasn't sold.' The moment you spoke it moved. Hold on to the word you spoke; don't depend on what your eyes tell you. See with the eye of faith.

Mountains move

I was teaching at a conference on speaking to the mountain. The Holy Spirit told me to let the people put it into practice there and then. I invited anybody who had a mountain that needed to be cast into the sea to find a space in the auditorium where they could stand. Many responded. I then told them, when they were ready, to speak to that obstacle in their path and it would go. It was a marvellous sight to see the people of God exercising their faith in such a way.

A few days later I received a call from the church leader who was hosting the conference. He told me that a lady from his church had been present with us and had responded to my invitation to deal with these mountains. Just prior to the conference she had been diagnosed with breast cancer but had told nobody except her husband. As she heard the teaching on faith, her own faith began to grow. When I called people out she joined them and spoke to the cancer in her body, commanding it to go from her as she exercised her mustard seed faith. Nobody laid hands on her; nobody else knew of her mountain.

When she returned to her home a letter was waiting for her; it was from her doctor. All trace of the cancer had disappeared!

The God who did it for that lady is the same God who will do it for you.

CHAPTER ELEVEN

The power of agreement

I tell you, that if two of you on earth agree about anything you ask for, it will be done for you by my Father in heaven. For where two or three come together in my name, there I am with them. (Jesus, in Matthew 18:19-20)

These words of Jesus unlock for us a powerful principle of confession within the *Circle of Life*. Remember that we have already discovered the creative and destructive power of words; and that when we confess we are literally saying the same words as God. We are agreeing with him and are thus bringing things into being. Abraham called himself what God called him — the father of many nations — even before he was. Something was created by his agreeing with God. I will keep reminding you of this fact.

This principle is at work here too, only this time we are agreeing with other people in their faith declarations. First we have to dispel some false notions about this passage. Jesus is not giving us an open cheque book to find someone to agree with us about just anything we want: a million pounds; that Ferrari we always longed for; the luxury vacation we can't afford. This principle of faith is meant to be practised for bringing into being things that the Father wants done in the name of the Son. We are agreeing on his will for something. Neither is this passage an excuse for small churches: 'Well, brother, there might only be the two of us who could be bothered to be here;

but where two or three are gathered...' It's nothing to do with that at all. Jesus is talking about releasing the will of God, not justifying smallness of thinking and minimal expectations.

God agrees with Himself

The principle of agreement originates in the godhead. It's vital we state that because it helps us focus the reason for such agreement among us as the people of God. God always speaks to himself and to us concerning his purpose; he doesn't speak idle words. We can see this in scriptures such as Genesis 1:26, where God (the word is *Elohim*) says, *'Let us'*. To whom is God speaking? He is speaking to himself. There is a divine conversation going on here between the three Persons of the Trinity about his purpose. The same principle of agreeing for purpose is demonstrated when God commissioned Isaiah:

> *'Whom shall I send? And who will go for us?' (Isaiah 6:8)*

Every conversation in the Trinity is the agreement of the one God in three Persons. Each action is the outcome of these conversations. Imagine the Father and Son agreeing about creating the world and the Holy Spirit saying, 'No, I don't think it will work'. That is an utter impossibility. God agrees with himself on everything; he is a covenant who always agrees. Everything that comes from the mouth of God is an agreement of the three Persons. God is a God who makes covenant because he **is** a covenant.

That's why God was so concerned when he came to look at the people who were building the tower of Babel. Notice what God said about them:

> *'If as one people they have begun to do this, then nothing they plan will be impossible for them.' (Genesis 11:6)*

Even these evil people would have succeeded for one simple reason: they agreed with each other. That is scary and awesome. They had learned the power of agreement because the one they ultimately served (the devil) knows what it can achieve. Just think:

if God gets his people to agree like this, only for the good of his purpose, what could they achieve?

Agreeing with one another is another example of the Law of Establishment: that a matter is established by two three witnesses. In this case the three witnesses who work together are God, you and the person you agree with concerning a matter. You could also say that the two witnesses on earth establish what the first witness in heaven is intending to perform. Whichever way you look at it, the power of agreement will release on the earth the will of Heaven.

There are two facets of the power of agreement that I want to get over to you:

1. The lifestyle of agreement

I constantly aim to ensure that only words of life and faith ever come out of my mouth. I want to be speaking words of truth that people can agree with. I have to create the environment for others to speak their agreement into. Therefore, I am not a quiet person; I am a confessor. I behave like this wherever I am, not just in church meetings. Since I am giving thanks in all circumstances I tend to speak a lot. Non Christian friends say I have a sunny disposition. This is not to blow my own trumpet but sometimes people I meet for business purposes tell me I have made their day. Just the way I speak affects them.

If you are next to me or near me in a meeting you will always find that if I hear someone say something that I agree with, I say so. I speak out my agreement: *'That's right'*, *'Amen'*, *'Yes'*, *'I agree'*. This can be if they pray, read the Word, are preaching, giving testimonies. If what this person is saying is in line with the truth of God and his Word, I will always speak my agreement. Those who know me will testify to this; I constantly speak agreement with truth. In doing that the speaker and I are agreeing with each other on earth and with God in heaven. As a result things are established in us and for us. I become what I agree with. I have trained myself to behave this way.

Amen!

That word *Amen* is important. Sometimes you hear it spoken in desperation to the preacher: 'Amen', meaning 'Please stop now, you're boring me and you've been droning on and on for over an hour. Amen. Let me out of here.' Or we use it to close our meetings; it's the sign we can all finally go home.

But it doesn't mean that. Amen means *'so be it, it is done.'* It is linked to the biblical term for faithfulness and truth. Where our modern versions have Jesus saying, 'I tell you the truth' that phrase in the Greek is actually *'Amen, Amen.'* Jesus is emphasising his words with a double agreement of what he is about to say: 'it is true, it is true.'

When Jesus spoke to the church at Laodicea he called himself the Amen:

> *These are the words of the Amen, the faithful and true witness, the ruler of God's creation. (Revelation 3:14)*

He challenged the church to agree with him about what he said concerning their state. It's only when you agree with God and see things from his viewpoint that you have any hope for the future. Look at this verse too:

> *For no matter how many promises God has made, they are "Yes" in Christ. And so through him the "Amen" is spoken by us to the glory of God." (2Corinthians 1:20)*

Whenever we hear something that is true — and Jesus is the Truth — we are designed to speak a creative word of agreement with it. In the moment we agree with that word of faith, when we give our 'Amen,' God works something in us and he releases the very thing we are agreeing into being for us. Speaking our agreement with others is a tremendously helpful habit in the process of hearing and believing. We **hear** somebody speak a truth; we **believe** it; we **confess** it in our agreement; we hear ourselves speak it; we believe what we speak. The seedbed of faith in our hearts is thus fertilised with more faith.

It also benefits the one who has spoken the word of faith to us. As we agree with them they hear their own words reaped back to them in a greater dimension than they sowed them. Everything we sow comes back in greater measure, including our words. So the person's faith is increased by our confession of their words. We all benefit!

Silence speaks

I've already told you that silence also speaks. If I don't respond in agreement to a word of faith then none of the above will happen for me; I have cut off a lifeline to the seedbed of faith in my heart. I certainly won't benefit and the one who spoke the word to me will not gain the full blessing intended for them in reaping back their words. I believe our silence actually says, 'I don't agree.' How can I know you agree if you don't say so? When I preach the first thing I usually say is, 'God is good.' I can tell by the response who is in life and who is not. If the response is 'Amen, all the time, yes he is, I agree,' somebody has been teaching these people well. If it's patchy or as silent as a graveyard, I have a lot of work to do.

I am not trying to get people just to repeat things after me like a variation on that children's game 'Simon says.' But I have been in situations where to get a Christian just to agree a truth from the Word of God is like pulling teeth. I believe the devil has put a muzzle over their mouths and is slowly suffocating them. There's a description of people we sometimes use: they are the strong silent type. According to the Word of God such people are not strong at all: they are weak. Others say they are shy: I tell them, 'Are you going to stand before God on Judgement Day and tell him the reason you never opened your mouth in biblical confession was because you were shy?'

The God who spoke the world into being is living in us and we are too afraid to speak because we are shy! You say, 'Roger, you're being hard on us.' No, I'm trying to help you. When I was young I was painfully shy. How could I fulfil God's plan for my life if I were like that today? I had to change.

The power of testimony

> *The accuser of our brothers, who accuses them before our God day and night, has been hurled down. They overcame him by the blood of the Lamb and by the word of their testimony. (Revelation 12:10-11)*

I love a good story. And there are no better stories than those that millions of Christians can recount every day about the wonderful things God does in our lives. Each day he saves, heals, restores, rescues, does miracles, achieves the impossible, meets all our needs, transforms communities, sets captives free, prospers the poor, guides us, rescues us — and so much more!

Our testimonies are weapons against the devil. He hates them as much as he hates the wonderful blood of Jesus. Our testimonies speak of God's faithfulness and power. They expose the lies and innuendos of the devil. They also are meant to encourage our fellow believers. We hear the story of what God has done for somebody and we say, 'he will do it for me.' That's why in our church meetings we always make room for testimonies, to give people ample opportunity to give glory to God and to say thank you to Jesus for what he has done. It builds up the faith of the saints when they hear such testimonies.

My son James was about to start a Masters Degree, but he had not received any funding. He needed about £3,000. He believed that God wanted him to do the course, and he had received confirmation from his leaders. But with only four days to enrolment he did not have a penny for his fees. His confession remained constant: that the Lord would provide for him. On this particular day James was attending a Leaders' conference and various brothers were giving testimony. One brother stood up and said, 'I want to praise the Lord that he has provided me with all my fees for my Masters Degree.' James was thrilled for his friend; and as the rest of us applauded the Lord's provision for this brother, James spoke to the Lord and said, 'Lord, you did it for him; thanks that you will do it for me too.' He didn't get up and announce his need to anybody; he just did it quietly. Later in the day another brother approached James and said the Lord had told him to pay all his fees. My son was truly blessed.

The next day another brother came to him and said the same thing! James told this second brother that he already had his need met; but the man insisted, since he had intended to do so for a long time. James accepted the offer. He then rang the first brother to release him from his commitment. The brother thanked James for calling, but said, 'Well I am blessed the other brother is meeting your need, but the Lord told me to as well. So I am still giving you what I promised.' God had not only supplied my son's entire need; he also blessed him above and beyond so he could sow out again.

The power of a man's testimony had released the faith of my son to receive a miracle.

2. Make agreements

The second aspect of the power of agreement is actually making agreement with someone over an issue. Jesus said that we should do this:

> *If two of you on earth agree about anything you ask for, it will be done for you by my Father in heaven. (Matthew 18:19)*

Let me repeat myself here: this is not a technique just to get what we want. It's releasing the will of heaven in the earth, even though it might well involve the everyday things of life. My wife Dianne often moves in this dimension of faith. As she has agreed in faith with others she has seen jobs provided for them; houses that had been on the market for ages sold; babies born to infertile couples (including twins!); diseases healed; and those who thought they would never marry find their partner. She doesn't engage in long drawn out counselling sessions and prayers. As she talks with people the Holy Spirit suddenly quickens her and she can tell that the person is in faith and ready to agree. She takes their hand and makes the agreement with them in a very specific way. There is no panic; she knows it's done on earth and in heaven. The outcome is assured.

Peter's Story

In June 2004 I was in conversation with a lovely couple from India who had just begun attending our church - Peter and his wife Jane (not their real names). They had been in the UK a while. They were living in Cardiff but Peter, who is a Pharmacist, could not get a post here. So he was working in the south of England, about 200 miles away. He could only get home at weekends, which was no good for the family. Furthermore, he was always kept on a temporary contract, so he couldn't get a mortgage.

As we talked I felt the Holy Spirit begin to stir me to challenge them to agree with me some things about their situation. So I asked Peter and Jane what was their heart's desire. They said they really wanted to be in Cardiff and to be in the church with us. They were convinced it was the will of God for them, to be planted in a good church and to have a proper home for the family. Then I asked him specifically what kind of job he wanted; he replied, 'a Pharmacist.' Then I asked, 'Which hospital?' He said 'The Heath' (the biggest hospital in our city). Next question: 'When do you want the job?' Reply: 'by the end of September 2004.'

I took Peter by the hand and we looked each other in the eye. I said, 'Peter, right now we are agreeing on earth concerning all these things, and the Lord will do it for us:

1. You will have a job as a Pharmacist;
2. It will be in the Heath Hospital, Cardiff;
3. You will have it by the end of September 2004.'

As I said each one, he spoke a word of faith agreement with me and God - 'amen'. I then turned to Jane and said, 'Start house-hunting.' Then God went to work.

In the middle of September Peter came up to me to tell me that each of the three things we had agreed on had happened; and he was starting work at the end of the month! I got him to tell the story to the church.

When he did he was very honest, because it transpired that after we had agreed together he had begun to apply for Pharmacist's jobs at the Heath, but also at other Cardiff hospitals. Some of the other hospitals had offered him interviews, but he received only refusals from the Heath. What should he do? He felt the Holy Spirit speak strongly to him that he should hold on to what we agreed. He declined the 'non-Heath' interviews.

Eventually he got an interview at the Heath for an ideal job. But he didn't get it and the time we had set was fast approaching. Then 'out of the blue' Peter got a call from the Heath, saying that they would like to offer him a job. It turned out to be an even better one than the one he didn't get. And he was to start at the end of September.

Within three months of starting the job Peter was given a significant increase in his salary. This continued for some more months; blessing flowed after him. He now has the job he wanted and more, and a lovely home. That was the will of God for him; that he could be with his family and make a home for them. All we did was agree in faith on it. God did the rest.

The never ending story

When Peter gave his testimony to the church another couple heard it. They were in a similar situation, only they were Nigerians in the process of moving from London and both needed new jobs. They came to me after the meeting and said, 'God did it for them; he will do it for us too. Let's agree.' We did; and you can guess the rest.

CHAPTER TWELVE

The power of disagreement

They did not go in because of their unbelief. (Hebrews 4:6)

This chapter might well be the most important one in the book for you. If there is one area of the *Circle of Life* that Christians miss out on more than the others it's this one. I am constantly amazed at some of the things that come out of the mouths of God's people. I'm not talking about swearing or cursing; I'm talking about the vast dictionaries of negativity that they have stored up in their hearts and which pour out of them all the time.

The power of disagreement

We have learnt that in order to live the life of faith we must operate the principle of the power of agreement. We also have to learn the power of **dis**agreement. That doesn't mean we become disagreeable or rude. We don't adopt an argumentative and combative attitude to people: it means we have to learn to **say no to unbelief** whenever it tries to nullify our faith. Sadly, too many times those words of unbelief will come through the words of God's people who speak with such negativity.

I believe that this principle of disagreement is so vital, because as I have stated on several occasions so far **our confession determines our destiny and our inheritance**.

If we confess that Jesus is Lord and believe in our heart that God raised him from the dead, we are saved. Our confession determines where we will spend eternity: in heaven or in hell. If you have never confessed Jesus as Lord then you're hell bound. If you have, then heaven is your destiny.

I trust that by now you have learnt the importance of your confession: that your words are creative, and things happen when you speak faith. But your words can also be just as destructive if you speak the negative words that Satan wants you to speak (remember what we had to say about this when we examined the two voices). Proverbs 18:21 says, *'the tongue has the power of life **and death**.'* Satan always speaks words of death and he wants you to do the same. He is unable to steal your destiny if you have confessed Jesus as Lord, but he wants to spoil your inheritance. He does that by getting you to speak unbelief. And so many Christians do his work for him.

It is appalling what comes out of the mouths of Christians, in direct contradiction with what the Word of God says. I hear them say that God lets them down, that the Word of God doesn't work, that they are terrible sinners, that they will never recover from illness, that God won't answer their prayer. I have even known Christians talk themselves into their graves. Yet God's people think it's acceptable to speak like this. I remember one person saying to me, 'Oh, God and I are not on speaking terms right now,' as if God were a friend they just fell out with in the schoolyard.

'You have a demon'

John chapter 8 is one of the most important passages in the Bible. It is a dialogue between Jesus and the Pharisees about who he is and it culminates in that earth shattering statement by the young carpenter from Nazareth:

> *'Amen, Amen, before Abraham was born I am!' (John 8:58).*

Just before Jesus made that incredible declaration the Pharisees repeatedly questioned him about his origins and accused him of all sorts of things, even that he was illegitimate. At one point they said this to Jesus:

> *'We know that you are a Samaritan and demon-possessed' (John 8:48).*

Powerful words indeed, laced with a deathly poison. But they didn't frighten Jesus. Nevertheless Jesus still decided to respond to these words. He didn't let them pass by unchallenged. He didn't agree with them; he didn't consider the possibility that he did have a demon and arrange to have a course of counselling. He didn't ask the Pharisees to qualify their statement. These words were in direct opposition to the truth of who Jesus was, so he operated the power of disagreement:

> *'I am not possessed by a demon', said Jesus, 'but I honour my Father and you dishonour me.' (John 8:49)*

This is the power of disagreement in action. He got to the core straight away: 'You are wrong. I cannot and will not accept what you say. That is not who I am.'

We have to act just like Jesus in this way whenever anything that is untrue and contrary to the Word of God is said to us. It must not find room in our hearts. We have to rebut it as soon as it flies towards our ears. We have to learn to say no to anything that seeks to bring unbelief or doubt into the seedbed of faith in our hearts. Remaining silent will not suffice either: we have to speak that disagreement. If we don't refuse it then rest assured it will get in, and eventually the overflow of the heart will speak it out in unbelief. The *Circle of Life* has been broken.

This idea of Christians as wimps, who won't say boo to a goose, is a total fallacy. Life is battle of words and the winner controls you.

'I am not a grasshopper'

It would help right now if you read Numbers 13 and 14; it's a frightening and awesome account of a whole generation of God's people who lost their inheritance because of their unbelief. They failed to disagree when they heard men speak words that were contrary to what God had spoken. Those words reached in to their hearts and overflowed in their own words of unbelief. God heard them and made a judgement that doomed them.

God instructed Moses to send twelve spies into Canaan to explore it. God had told them he had given them this land:

The LORD said to Moses, 'Send some men to explore the land of Canaan, which I am giving to the Israelites.' (Numbers 13:1-2)

These men had heard the Word of God: the land was theirs. All they had to do was explore it and discover some more details about the towns and cities and the condition of the land (13:17-20). For the next forty days they went through the land and it was just as Moses had said. They even brought back some of the fruit of the land, a large bunch of grapes. God's word was true; he had kept his promise. They even had physical evidence. The problem started when ten of these spies opened their mouths; their confession would cost them and a whole generation of their listeners dear:

They gave Moses this account: "We went into the land to which you sent us, and it does flow with milk and honey! Here is its fruit. But the people who live there are powerful, and the cities are fortified and very large. We even saw descendants of Anak there. The Amalekites live in the Negev; the Hittites, Jebusites and Amorites live in the hill country; and the Canaanites live near the sea and along the Jordan." (Numbers 13:27-29)

They started well: 'yes, you're right; the land does flow with milk and honey.' But then everything fell apart: 'But....' These men spoke words of death that were totally contrary to the Word of God. He had said the land was theirs; no matter that it was already inhabited. God had given the land to his people, but these men had begun to spread a bad report. In spite of what God had said they refused to believe and told their fellow Israelites they could not go in and take the land. Instead of disagreeing, the rest of the people began to agree, even if they remained silent.

What happened next determined the destiny and inheritance of two men: Joshua and Caleb, the other two spies. As soon as Caleb heard what was being said and saw the effect it was having on the people he stepped forward:

> *Caleb silenced the people before Moses and said, "We should go up and take possession of the land, for we can certainly do it." (Verse 30)*

Caleb said, 'I disagree with this unbelief. We can do this, because God spoke to us, he has given it to us, it's ours. We just have to take possession of the land. Let's go and take it; don't agree with these men of unbelief.' His words saved him and ensured his destiny and inheritance. Joshua stood with Caleb and agreed with his confession (Numbers 14:6-9). But the confession of the ten spies won the day:

> *The men who had gone up with him said, "We can't attack those people; they are stronger than we are." And they spread among the Israelites a bad report about the land they had explored. They said, "The land we explored devours those living in it. All the people we saw there are of great size. We saw the Nephilim there... We seemed like grasshoppers in our own eyes, and we looked the same to them." (Numbers 13:31-33)*

What a confession! 'We are nothing but grasshoppers.' The tragedy was that the whole community chose to believe the ten men of unbelief and agree with them. They refused to believe God and agree with him and his two witnesses, Joshua and Caleb. The people's refusal to believe God and their subsequent confession of that unbelief cost them their inheritance. In a harrowing passage of Scripture God condemned all those over twenty years old who had left Egypt to die in the desert. He spoke a word of judgement to them all:

> *'Not one of them will ever see the land I swore on oath to their forefathers. No one who has treated me with contempt will ever see it.' (Numbers 14:23)*

However, because Joshua and Caleb disagreed with the unbelief of the whole community they were the only people over twenty years old who did inherit the land, almost forty years later. A whole generation lost their inheritance. The other ten spies didn't last long and died pretty swiftly (Numbers 14:37). They paid a massive for those words of unbelief.

That is incredible, don't you think? I don't want to frighten you, but we have to be just as ruthless in the church with the unbelief that dribbles out of our mouths. Jesus was ruthless with it when accused of being demon-possessed. It's just as important you do the same when people speak like that to you. Don't keep quiet; say something. Disagree. Your silence means you agree.

'I'm a nothing'

A couple of years ago Dianne and I were speaking at a conference. At one of the sessions, the meeting seemed to be coming to an end and was winding down. I was not the speaker at this session, and was sitting there, listening to the Spirit. It was clear that something was about to happen. One of the other men there, a friend of mine and a leader in a church, got up and began to express what he was feeling the Lord wanted to do. He said, 'I am only a pleb, but....' Now a *pleb* is a term for a common person, someone of little or no importance, of insignificance. Suddenly I found myself on my feet and in front of the whole conference I said, 'Excuse me, there are no plebs in this room, only children of the living God.' This man is older than me; I love him and respect him. But here I was; I could not let that pass, it would have got into the people. If this man were a pleb and a leader, what were they? It wasn't true; he is not a pleb.

He stared across the room at me for what felt like an eternity. I calmly held his gaze, and then he said, 'You are right. I am sorry; I should never have said such a thing.' My friend is a real man of God.

Don't talk like that

You might think I'm being over the top, but I'm not. If you say things around me or to me that are not true of God or you, I'm not going to let you get away with it. Your inheritance is at stake. That's why sometimes I'll stop people in their tracks and say, 'I am sorry, but what you are saying about yourself is not true. You are not a worm, you are not a failure, you are a wonderful work of art, fashioned by your heavenly Father.' I have to counteract the unbelief that they are speaking into their seedbed.

Now let me say this. Living in disagreement with unbelief does not mean that I never face reality. Abraham faced the fact that his body was good as dead (Romans 4:19). He said to God and himself, 'I am old; my body is not that of an athlete.' He faced it, but he put his faith in what God had said. He did not give into the facts of his bodily condition; he agreed with God and what God had said about his situation: 'you will have a son.'

I have had to do the same. In July 2005 I had a heart attack: that is a fact. I had it. It was real and very painful. But even when walking through that valley of the shadow of death I was not going to agree with voices of unbelief from anywhere. And do you know what happened? The doctors and nurses, none of whom was a Christian, all spoke faith to me. They said the operation was a great success; they told me that I would make a complete recovery. They said that I would be stronger than before. None of them told me I would die.

All the cards I received, every email, every message on my answering machine, was the same. Faith, faith, faith. Don't ever come to me and say things like, 'Well, Roger, life won't be the same again. No more energetic preaching for you, no more excitement, just calm down.' I will not listen to such drivel: I choose to believe the Word of God and I believe in a God of restoration! I actually refused to let some people come and visit me because I knew that they would bring negative speaking with them. I kept them away. My life was at stake.

I am not advocating that we speak in some charismatic psychobabble of unreality. But we have to learn that what comes out of our mouths determines our destiny and our inheritance. It also determines how we live every day. If we grasp this principle of disagreement then our churches will be healthier places to live; our homes will be full of peace instead of war; and God's people will realise that we are the healing of the nations.

CHAPTER THIRTEEN

Just do it

Do not merely listen to the word, and so deceive yourselves. Do what it says. (James 1:22)

It's time to move on to the fourth and final part of the *Circle of Life*. So far we have established that in order for us to live by faith we must develop the lifestyle of hearing, believing and confessing the Word of God. These things are natural for us to do as Christians, just like breathing. It's the way God has designed us to live as new creations in Christ.

But there's one more part that makes all the others effective, and without it they simply cannot function in the way they are intended. It's a very simple and straightforward aspect of the Circle, but it's the one that makes the others work.

Do the word; just do it.

It's imperative to get into the habit of constantly hearing God, believing what he tells you and confessing his word in agreement. The crunch comes when you put all those things into action: when you do your faith. It's only in the doing of your faith that your hearing, believing and confessing are proved to be real. When you put your faith into action the rubber hits the road and things happen.

Who's that stranger?

I love the letter of James in the New Testament; it's so down to earth and real. James doesn't beat around the bush in getting his point across, he tells it like it is, especially when it comes to having a doing faith:

> *Anyone who listens to the word but does not do what it says is like a man who looks at his face in a mirror and, after looking at himself, goes away and immediately forgets what he looks like. (James 1:23-24)*

James illustrates so brilliantly how stupid we are when we don't put our faith in action. Imagine you get up in the morning, go into the bathroom and see yourself in the mirror. You recognise the handsome face looking back at you as your own. You do what you have to do to it to make it ready for the day. When you get downstairs you see a photograph on the wall with four people in it: your wife, two children and a total stranger. You say to your wife, 'Darling, who's that strange man in this photo?' She looks over the table with a concerned look: 'It's you.' 'Never seen him before,' you reply. Despite your wife's remonstrations you continue to insist that the man in the photo is a complete stranger. Once she realises you're not joking she's on the phone to the doctor: you're seriously ill.

It's utterly ridiculous isn't it? But that's exactly what someone who succeeds in the first three areas of the Circle of Life but fails in the fourth is like.

Faith without action is not faith

The Bible says very clearly that faith without action is no faith at all. We can be constantly hearing the word; we can confess it till the cows come home; but unless or until we **do** what we hear, believe and confess, we've got nowhere.

That's how foolish (I use the word advisedly) we are if we never or only occasionally put our faith into practice. You see, faith without action is actually dead. Action is the proof of faith; and until we actually **do** something there is no basis at all for assuming that our faith is real. This is the very thing that James tackles in his letter:

Faith by itself, if it's not accompanied by action, is dead. (James 2:17)

Real faith will produce real actions. Hearing, believing and confessing the Word of God will result in a life of active faith. You are designed to be a doer.

Back to Abraham

Many times throughout this book I've used Abraham as an example of faith. It's good that we've been able to examine his life like that; after all, he's our father in the faith. We've discovered that he heard the word of God that he was going to have a son. He believed what God told him despite his circumstances. He confessed it for twenty four years and grew in faith all the time. As the years went by and he and Sarah got older and older he never wavered in his believing confession concerning what he had heard from God. But there was something else that Abraham and Sarah had to do. Now I don't want to sound crude or coarse here, but I have to state the obvious: Abraham and Sarah had to continue their physical relationship. This was the doing of their faith. There has only been one virgin birth, and it was not Isaac. He was conceived and born in the same way as everybody else.

If Abraham and Sarah had not continued the physical side of their marriage relationship, in faith that their action would produce what God had promised, then nothing would have happened. Isaac was born because of the promise of God and the faith of Abraham and Sarah, including their putting their faith into action by continuing to have a physical relationship.

'Sacrifice Isaac'

Abraham's faith was tested and proved real time and again in his life through his actions. This was especially so when God commanded him to sacrifice the son he had been waiting for all those years and who was the one through whom Abraham's offspring would bless the world.

Take time to read the story in Genesis 22:1-18 now; it will only take you a few minutes.

By this time Isaac was probably a teenager or even older. Years had passed since the miracle of Sarah's conception and the wonder of his birth. But now God came again to Abraham to test him in order for his faith to grow even more. He asked him to sacrifice Isaac. Immediately Abraham responded; all the hearing, believing, confessing of the previous years were put into practice again during those three days. He believed that if he killed Isaac then God would raise him from the dead. So he did what God told him; he put his faith into action:

> *Abraham was considered righteous for what he did when he offered his son Isaac on the altar…his faith and his actions were working together, and his faith was made complete by what he did. (James 2:21-22)*

> *By faith Abraham, when God tested him, offered Isaac as a sacrifice. He who had received the promises was about to sacrifice his one and only son, even though God had said to him, "It is through Isaac that your offspring will be reckoned." Abraham reasoned that God could raise the dead, and figuratively speaking, he did receive Isaac back from death. (Hebrews 11:17-19)*

Even though to the natural mind this command sounded crazy, Abraham understood that all he had to do was carry out the instruction: to sacrifice Isaac. He believed that the promise made concerning Isaac was still good and God would raise him from the dead. So he acted on the command: he **did** the word. He even strapped his son to the altar and was about to deal the death blow when God told him to stop. That's a doing faith. God requires the same active faith from us as he did from Abraham. It's easy to live this way; you just have to trust and act. God is behind his word to act as we act on it.

Just Do It

Dianne and I were visiting a church, teaching on the Holy Spirit. In one session the gifts of the Spirit were being exercised and imparted (see Romans 1:11). A certain young lady there wanted to begin laying hands on the sick and to move in gifts of healing. We laid hands on her, imparted to her and then encouraged her to start laying hands on sick people. Some months later we were in another church and this same young lady was present. In a similar session she came to us and asked us to pray for her once more, that she would start moving in the gifts of healing. I said to her, 'We already prayed this for you. Have you actually laid hands on anybody yet?' She replied, 'No, I haven't'. I asked, 'Have you met any sick people since we last saw you?' 'Of course', she answered. I said, 'Then all you have to do is lay your hands on them. Just do it'. We continued to encourage the lady in her faith, but we could not pray for her again to receive something she had already received but not done. Her hearing, believing and confessing would have no release until she actually laid her hands on a sick body. When she finally did, people were healed.

A lady in our church (we'll call her Mary) brought a friend of hers to me at a Sunday meeting. Jesus was moving powerfully in healing that morning, and the anointing of the Holy Spirit was very strong. As Mary approached me with her friend the Holy Spirit told me not to lay hands on the lady, but to get Mary to do it. I immediately recalled a meeting several months earlier where Mary had received a prophetic word that she would exercise the gift of healing in a significant manner, to which she responded with such faith and confession that she just broke before the Lord and spent a long time under the power of the Holy Spirit on the floor. As I spoke to the lady I noticed that Mary was standing next to her, shaking ever so slightly, rubbing her hands together. I said to the lady, 'I am not going to lay my hands on you, Mary will, and Jesus will heal you.' Mary looked at me, her eyes almost popping out of her head! But she did what I said, even though by now she was shaking like a leaf and looked like she needed healing herself. The moment her hands touched her friend, the lady fell to the ground and was immediately healed!

Later I spoke to Mary. She was as high as a kite. She reminded me of that earlier meeting and said, 'I've been waiting ever since that night to lay hands on someone. This is the first time I've done it!' Needless to say, it wasn't the last.

My Friend the Tither

A young man in our church struggled with tithing (bringing to God ten percent of our wealth). He had heard our teaching on it and believed the Bible teaches it (it does: for example, see Genesis 14:8-24; Malachi 3:6-12; Luke 11:42). He confessed he believed in it and he confessed that he should do it. But he never tithed. He looked at his bank account; it was always overdrawn. He was sliding further and further into debt, simply because he was robbing God. By the way, that's what you do when you don't tithe. It's God's money and you don't want to be stealing from God. It's not recommended and a dangerous thing to do.

This young man would come to me at regular intervals and I'd tell him that he actually had to tithe; just agreeing with it, believing in it, and confessing it would not work. God could not bless him until he unlocked the spiritual law of sowing and reaping by actually, physically bringing God the tithe. The devourer would continue to mess him up until he brought his tithe to the Lord (you don't give your tithe, you give your offering. The tithe is God's so you can't give him what already belongs to him; you bring what is actually already his to him).

Finally, one day he said 'Roger, I really want to tithe. Please help me.' 'OK,' I responded, 'This is what we'll do. You get paid this Friday. When you get your payslip, look at your gross salary. Calculate the tithe (10% is so easy - God is so kind to us. I'm glad he didn't say 7.35%!). Then write your cheque for that tithe amount and bring it on Sunday morning. When it's time for us to come forward to bring our tithes and give our offerings you come to me.' He did.

That Sunday at the appointed time he walked towards me with a mixture of excitement, faith and apprehension on his face. We walked to the baskets and as he held his tithe out I told him to thank God for being his source and then to do his faith by actually putting his tithe in the basket. He obeyed. Then I prayed for him and commanded the windows of heaven to pour out that blessing.

The next Sunday he came running up to me, beaming. He gushed, 'You'll never guess what happened!' He began to tell me all that had happened in his finances that week: he had received a pay increase, a tax refund, he had more money in his account than he thought, things he just could not explain. All this happened because he put his faith into action by actually bringing his tithe. Funny, but he has not struggled with tithing since. He is a really generous man.

All of it

By now I hope you're excited about the wonderful things about to be unleashed in your life as you grow in the four aspects of the *Circle of Life*, especially having a doing faith. You can see all those sick bodies being healed; praise the Lord!

But living by faith and doing the Word of God means doing **all** of it, not just the seemingly attractive parts. Jesus came to fulfil the whole Word of God, not merely the 'nice' parts. He came to fulfil Isaiah 61:

> *The Spirit of the Lord is on me, because he has anointed me to preach good news to the poor. He has sent me to proclaim freedom for the prisoners and recovery of sight for the blind, to release the oppressed, to proclaim the year of the Lord's favour. (Luke 4:18-19)*

Exciting and exhilarating stuff! But he also came to fulfil scriptures like this one:

> *He was pierced for our transgressions, he was crushed for our iniquities; the punishment that brought us peace was upon him, and by his wounds we are healed. (Isaiah 53:5)*

Jesus didn't pick and choose which parts of the Word he would act on: he acted on it all. That same principle holds for us too as we live the *Circle of Life*. It means I lay hands on the sick and I tithe; I forgive my brother when he sins against me; I live free from condemnation; I never gossip. I love with the love of God; I treat my wife and children in the way the Word of God says I should.

If we just do whatever the Word says, it must work. The Word of God is God's integrity. Take him at his word; put your faith into action and just do whatever the Word says.

Just do it.

CHAPTER FOURTEEN

Whatever

Whatever he tells you to do, do it. (John 2:5)

When we put our faith into action — when we do our faith — we have to be careful that we do so in obedience to God. Sometimes the Holy Spirit will ask us to do something that seems unreasonable or irrational to us, even though everything he asks us to do is always in line with the nature of God and his Word. It is a test of our faith to see if we will respond in obedience or whether we will complain, draw back through fear, or just plain refuse to do it. This is what happened to the Old Testament people of God at Meribah, where God tested their faith when the water ran out (see Exodus 17:1-7 and Psalm 81:7). The people failed the test of faith and obedience.

Why is obedience so important?

Obedience proves our faith

> *We received grace and apostleship to call people from among all the Gentiles to the obedience that comes from faith. (Romans 1:5).*

First, obedience is the proof our faith in Jesus as Lord. If our faith in him is genuine then we will naturally obey him. If there is no faith in us then we will not obey him. That is why water baptism is so important; the very first proof of our faith in Jesus as Lord is demonstrated in our being baptised in water straight away. It is never given as an option in the New Testament; it is always a command (see Acts 2:38-41; Acts 10:48). If you are unwilling to be baptised there is a question over the genuineness of your faith. That's just the way it is.

Obedience proves our discipleship

> *Then Jesus came to them and said, "All authority in heaven and on earth has been given to me. Therefore go and make disciples of all nations, baptising them in the name of the Father and of the Son and of the Holy Spirit, and teaching them to obey everything I have commanded you. And surely I am with you always, to the very end of the age." (Matthew 28:18-20)*

Jesus did not come to make converts: he came to make disciples. That word 'disciple' means a follower or a learner. Discipleship is a lifelong process of following Jesus and learning more of him. The proof of our discipleship is if we obey what we are taught.

Obedience proves whether we love Jesus

> *If you love me, you will obey what I command. (John 14:15)*

Jesus makes a very simple and stark statement here: if we love him we will obey what he commands us. If we don't obey him then we don't love him, no matter what we say. Remember, we have to have a doing faith; and we do exactly what and only what the Master tells us, because we love him.

Obedience proves who we serve

> *Don't you realise that whatever you choose to obey becomes your master? You can choose sin, which leads to death,*

or you can choose to obey God and receive his approval. (Romans 6:16, NLT)

Jesus said we cannot serve two Masters (Matthew 6:24). Whatever or whoever I obey is my Master. I can obey Jesus; then he is my Master. I can obey my own will; the devil is my Master. Whoever has control of me is the one who gets my obedience.

Obedience is Necessary

Obedience not only proves us, it is also extremely necessary, for one simple reason. Disobedience was the reason and the issue of the Fall of Adam. He willingly and deliberately chose to disobey God, in spite of hearing God's clear instructions and warnings. He obeyed the voice of the devil, who is

The mighty prince of the power of the air. He is the spirit at work in the hearts of those who refuse to obey God. (Ephesians 2:2)

The catastrophic result of Adam's wilful disobedience to the clear spoken word and will of God was the entry of sin into the world:

Through the disobedience of the one man the many were made sinners. (Romans 5:19)

But praise God! There was another who did obey:

Through the obedience of the one man the many will be made righteous. (Romans 5:19)

Jesus was a total contrast to Adam. Where Adam disobeyed and brought sin and unrighteousness into the world, Jesus was completely obedient in everything and brought righteousness to all who believe and obey. That is why the Word of God says of Jesus:

> *'Here I am— it is written about me in the scroll— I have come to do your will, O God.' (Hebrews 10:7)*

And this obedient Son taught us to pray,

> *'Our Father in heaven...your kingdom come, your will be done on earth as it is in heaven'. (Matthew 6:9-10).*

That's the prayer of faith and obedience.

Obedient Faith and Disobedient Unbelief

The Word of God contains many examples of those who obeyed and those who disobeyed, along with the outcome and consequence of both. Let's look at one of each: Saul, who disobeyed; and Rahab, who obeyed.

The Example of King Saul

Before continuing, it would be really helpful for you to read the whole of 1Samuel 15. As you read make a note of the specific word of command that Saul received to obey and what he did with it. Note especially verses 22-23.

God was very gracious to Saul. He sent the prophet Samuel with a very clear command and the reason for that command. Saul had to destroy the Amalekites completely, along with all their possessions, because of what they had done to Israel (verses 2-3). The Word of God was very clear and very simple. Saul started well; he set out on the task. But when it came time to actually do what he had been told he did not do it: he refused to kill the enemy King and the best of the livestock. He disobeyed, and imposed his own ideas, preferences and agenda on God's will.

Now look at his downfall. In verse 13 he began by lying: 'I have carried out the Lord's instructions.' What a bare faced lie. Samuel immediately exposed him; so Saul's next ploy was to blame others (verse 15). That failed, and Samuel laid it all on the table when he challenged Saul, 'Why didn't you obey the Lord?' By now Saul knew he was in trouble so he tried to play the religious card:

'I kept the best animals to sacrifice them to the Lord your God.' (verse 21)

That was the final straw for Samuel and for God. In one of the most withering Old Testament passages Samuel condemned Saul to his fate:

Does the LORD delight in burnt offerings and sacrifices as much as in obeying the voice of the LORD? To obey is better than sacrifice, and to heed is better than the fat of rams. For rebellion is like the sin of divination, and arrogance like the evil of idolatry. Because you have rejected the word of the LORD, he has rejected you as king. (1Samuel 15:22-23)

Finally, Saul came clean, but it was too late. He admitted that the fear of man had caused him to disobey God. Peer pressure, the ambitions and aspirations of others, his own lack of the fear of God, caused him to disobey and he lost his throne. The consequences of this act of disobedient unbelief were catastrophic for Saul. He wasted his destiny. God replaced him with a different kind of King:

After removing Saul, God made David their king. He testified concerning him: 'I have found David son of Jesse a man after my own heart; he will do everything I want him to do.' (Acts 13:22)

The Example of Rahab

Rahab's story begins in Joshua chapter 2. She was a prostitute: not a naturally good start. But God is a God of grace and mercy (always remember that Paul of Tarsus was a murderer before God got hold him). As an act of kindness Rahab sheltered the two spies who had sneaked into Jericho to explore it before the Israelites attacked. She knew that God was with them and had heard of what he had done for them (verse 8-10). So she asked these men to show her the covenant faithful love of God (verse 12). She requested that she and her family would be spared from death in the attack.

The two spies agreed and told Rahab to do two specific things:

- She must tie a scarlet cord in her window;
- She must bring all her family into her house and not let anyone of them out during the onslaught.

Rahab agreed. There was only one problem:

The house she lived in was part of the city wall. (verse 15)

Oh dear, oh dear. This could have been written as a perfect Hollywood movie plot. The spies did not know what was going to happen to that wall; and Rahab certainly didn't. But she obeyed the word that the spies gave her.

The next we hear of Rahab is in chapter six of Joshua. After the Israelites had marched around the city each day Joshua finally gave the command. The trumpets sounded and the people shouted (note the power of the spoken word. The wall collapsed at their shout of agreement). As we all know, at this sound the wall fell down – with Rahab and her family still inside it. Now the Bible doesn't tell us what was going in the house while all this was taking place. Nevertheless we can easily imagine the scene: a whole family gathered together for safety when suddenly the very thing they thought was going to be their salvation began falling down around their ears. What should they do? Run for their lives? Get out as fast as they could? It was completely understandable and the natural thing to do. Those spies had broken their promise. Rahab had been betrayed. What could you expect from such people? Let's get out of here.

But they didn't do any of those things. Joshua 6:23 tells us that Rahab and all her family were still in what was left of the house, along with the scarlet cord, that was still hanging out of the window. She and her whole family survived because they obeyed the Word of God. In spite of all that contradicted it, Rahab kept the family in the house. She trusted the oath of the spies, and therefore she trusted God and his word. She acted on it to the letter. Even when the pressure of the situation demanded that she abandon the house and run for her life, she refused to disobey. Why? She had faith and proved it in her obedience. She did the whatever.

The consequences of Rahab's faith and obedience are truly amazing. She is in the list of the great heroes of the faith in Hebrews 11:

> *By faith the prostitute Rahab...was not killed with those who were disobedient. (Hebrews 11:31)*

But more than that: look in Matthew 1:5 and you will see that this woman, because of her faith and her obedience became an ancestor of King David and therefore one of the human ancestors of the Saviour of the World, Jesus Christ. Now that is what I call a fulfilled destiny. Yours is just as significant.

CHAPTER FIFTEEN

Long life

With long life will I satisfy him. (Psalm 91:16)

Until 8th July 2005 I had never been seriously ill my whole life. I was fit and in the best of health. I ate well, was not overweight, and exercised regularly. In fact, just the day before I had run two miles, something I did a few times a week.

Just after 8 a.m. that day it all changed. I was driving home after taking Dianne to work when suddenly I felt absolutely dreadful. I had no idea what was wrong with me; I thought it was acute indigestion but the pain was awful. I managed to drive the rest of the way home and collapsed on to the bed. I stuffed myself with antacid pills but after an hour or so the pain was increasing and I was getting weaker. I didn't realise that I was having a heart attack.

'You're having a heart attack'

My son James was home that morning and after speaking on the phone to my friend Doctor Richard Pemberton, he persuaded me to go to my local General Practitioner. James came with me. The staff were tremendous and in a few minutes the nurse was examining me with an ECG machine. She took the results to the doctor and the next thing I heard was the sound of running down the corridor towards the room I was in. The doctor burst in and said words that I never expected to hear: 'Mr Aubrey, you're in the middle of a massive heart attack. The ambulance is on its way.' She began to work on me while James sat next to me; he was amazing. I turned to him and said, 'I'm not going anywhere. This is not my day to die.' He looked at me and spoke back his agreement. Then he asked the doctor if we could be alone together to pray. James laid his hands on me and prayed a prayer of faith about my life and my future. Even though I was quite weak I spoke out my agreement. I was determined not to die. It's marvellous to have children like that.

A few minutes later the paramedics arrived and I was absolutely blown away to see that out of all the ambulance crews in the city the Lord had sent me a brother from the church whose name is Rob. He was just as surprised to see me! God had sent me a man of God to look after me. Rob and his partner got to work straight away and in a few moments I was in the back of the ambulance on the way to hospital.

A long life

As I lay there the Holy Spirit began to speak to me. Some of the things he said are personal to me but one thing he spoke was from the Word of God:

> *You will not fear the terror of night, nor the arrow that flies by day, nor the pestilence that stalks in the darkness, nor the plague that destroys at midday. A thousand may fall at your side, ten thousand at your right hand, but it will not come near you. (Psalm 91:5-7)*

At that moment, in the back of an ambulance, wired up to heart monitors, I had a choice: to believe what the Word of God said to me or to let this circumstances take over and be terrified. The Holy Spirit spoke to me again:

> *"Because he loves me," says the LORD, "I will rescue him; I will protect him, for he acknowledges my name. He will call upon me, and I will answer him; I will be with him in trouble, I will deliver him and honour him. With long life will I satisfy him and show him my salvation." (Psalm 91:14-16)*

Through the oxygen mask I managed to croak: 'Lord, I believe you. I will live a long satisfied life.' Immediately a wave of peace came over me and I knew that even though I was walking through the valley of the shadow of death the Lord was with me and would bring me out the other side. I just knew it.

That evening, after I had been operated on by a wonderful team I lay in the intensive care unit. My children James and Naomi had been to see me and were magnificent in their faith. My dear friend and spiritual father Keri Jones had visited to pray with me and encourage me with words of faith. Then Dianne and I had some time alone together. I asked her to read Psalm 91 to me. It was the very word that God had spoken to her when she received the call from James earlier in the day to tell he what had happened to me.

As Dianne read this incredible Psalm she paused at certain points and we agreed together that this word was true for us. There in the midst of the valley we were on the mountain.

The enemy pays a visit

I was in hospital for about a week and then had two months off to recover and recuperate. The night before I went home the enemy came calling. I doubt if it was the devil himself; he has bigger targets than me.

One morning the doctors told me that I would be going home the next day. That afternoon I was talking with some of the other patients on the ward and I said: 'Well, guys, I'm glad to be getting out of here tomorrow.' One of them, the joker in the pack, retorted, 'You won't be getting out tomorrow. You'll be here for ages yet. They've been telling me for days that I'm going home but when the day comes they always say I must stay a little longer.' I smiled at him and said, 'I'm going home tomorrow.' It was all good natured, but I traced another voice behind his, and I was not going to agree with it. He came back at me: 'I'm telling you there's no way you're going home tomorrow.' I replied: 'You just watch. I'm leaving here in the morning.'

That evening I was sitting on my bed reading my Bible when a young man called Paul (not his real name) was brought on to the ward and put in the bed next to mine. Once he was settled in we began to chat. It transpired that he was a Christian and he knew me. He had seen me reading the Bible and recognised me, having visited our church and heard me preach. We had a really good time of fellowship, encouraging one another in the Lord.

Just after eleven that night as I was drifting off to sleep, Paul began to have a nasty turn. He was in great pain and got very distressed. The nurses came to him quickly but he was still writhing in agony. As I heard his cries a voice spoke to me: 'I'm going to kill him and I'm going to get you too.' I recognised the evil one. Another voice spoke: 'you will not fear the terror of night.' It was the Lord speaking Psalm 91:5 to me again. I got up from my bed and walked into the bathroom. I locked the door and sat on the edge of the bath. I spoke: 'Enemy, let me tell **you** something. You came at me with the arrow that flew by day. You didn't get me. And now you've come with the terror of night. You will not have me. And let me tell you something else: you will not have Paul either.'

Then I began to pray and thank God for delivering Paul and me. When I got back to the ward Paul was calming down as his pain subsided. Soon after he was back to normal and the nurses left him. He began to apologise for the noise he had made (he was a really godly man). I said, 'Paul, I just prayed for you while that was going on. You're going to be fine. In fact, I will be walking out of here tomorrow. You watch me go because you will walk out well too.'

'I'm going home'

That night I slept like a baby. Next morning I bathed and dressed, ready to go home. As I sat waiting for my release papers my sceptical friend wandered over and reminded me that I'd still be there the next day. I smiled and affirmed I was going home that day. About two hours later the doctor came to see me. He said, 'Well, Mr Aubrey, we're very pleased with your progress. Here are your release papers. We've called your wife; she's on her way to collect you. You can go home.' I could have kissed him.

Thirty minutes later Dianne walked on to the ward. I stood, took her arm and smiled at my sceptical friend. His jaw had dropped. I said, 'Goodbye, I'm going home.' Then I turned to Paul and said to him, 'Don't forget what I said. You'll leave here like I am doing now.' Then I walked out. I heard later that Paul is now fine.

In the following weeks and months as I recuperated I had to continue in the fourfold process of hearing, believing, confessing and doing. There were many times when I had to choose to hear and believe God's word and to confess my agreement with it. I had to put my faith into action. If I hadn't I could have been in my grave by now. Even after all this time I still have to live this way.

The *Circle of Life* works

I've told you this story because I want you to know that the things I have written about in this book are not empty theories to me. At my moment of crisis, when I was in grave danger, the *Circle of Life* that I have been living by for many years worked for me. When a circumstance arose and I did not have time to make major adjustments in my attitude or speech, the four parts of the circle – hearing, believing, confessing and doing – all kicked in and saved my life.

I am so grateful to God that he spared me. I know that these principles of living by faith work. I am living proof that God is faithful and worthy of your trust. I am convinced his word is utterly true and can be relied on to work for his people. I am not special and I have not discovered anything new here. Millions of God's people live this way; but it's the way **all** his people are designed to live.

Let me encourage you to begin to put these principles into practice. Don't worry if you make mistakes or fail along the way. See it as a way of life that you are going to adopt. It takes time to develop good habits. God is so gracious and he is always for you. He never condemns you. He wants you to succeed and refuses to write you off as a hopeless case. And as you get increasingly into the habit of hearing God, believing what he says, confessing his word and doing it, you are going to discover just how easy and natural it is.

It's just like breathing.